Thirty Days at the Foot of the Cross

Edited by
Thomas and Sheila Jones

Thirty Days at the Foot of the Cross

ISBN 978-1-948450-33-1

Printed in the United States of America.

Interior book design: Toney C. Mulhollan.

Cover design: Chris Costello.

Illumination Publishers titles may be purchased in bulk for classroom instruction, business, fund-raising, or sales promotional use. For information, please e-mail Paul Vasqeuz at paul.ipibooks@me.com.

Illumination Publishers cares deeply about using renewable resources and uses recycled paper whenever possible.

Published by Illumination Publishers, 6010 Pinecreek Ridge Court, Spring, Texas 77379-2513. www.ipibooks.com.

About the editors: Tom and Sheila Jones served as authors and editors at Discipleship Publications International and Good Book Press for many years.

Dedication

This book is dedicated to Cecil and Helen Wooten, two disciples whose inspiring hearts showed us so dramatically that it is never too late to come to the cross and make it the center of your life. We say thanks to them for all the ways they have lived before us.

CONTENTS

FOREWORD

Only When We See the Cross

For nearly two millennia Jesus Christ has been regarded as the most important person who ever lived. We set our calenders, our moral standards, and as his disciples, even the course of our lives by this God-man. But sadly, most who wear the name "Christian" do not really grasp the meaning and significance of the central event of history: his death on the cross.

In reality the cross is God's dagger in the heart of Satan, God's trap set from the beginning of time but sprung only in the fullness of time. Even in this we can become observers of the cross rather than active participants. Paul said that the message of the cross is the power of God (1 Corinthians 1:18). Only when we realize that we are the ones who deserve the punishment of the cross, that Jesus took our place, can God's power be released. Only when we are cut to the heart with the horrendousness of our sin and the magnitude of God's love, is the transforming power of the cross released. Only when we look to Jesus on the cross and see his surrender, do we understand his call for us to totally surrender, take up our cross daily and follow him. Then the real miracles of God begin in our lives, transforming us more and more into the likeness of Jesus!

Being impacted by the cross is not a one-time thing: It is lifetime thing. The cross can become stale and lose its emotional impact on us if we just view it rather than experience it. That is why I am encouraged by this book. Our time alone with God each morning sets the tone for the entire day, and this book provides a spiritual breakfast that will give energy all day long—a whole month's supply.

I personally know all of the writers. I have labored beside them in God's Kingdom—all of them have devoted themselves to God's work—and I know that they each draw their power from the message of the cross.

The thoughts here for each day are not some dry theological expositions, but they hit "where we live"; and they end with challenges to put the thoughts into practice so that we will have the life as well as the doctrine (1 Timothy 4:16). I enthusiastically recommend this book to you, and I pray you enjoy and are transformed by your time at the foot of the cross.

—Al Baird
Phoenix, Arizona, U.S.A.

INTRODUCTION

Thirty Days That Can Change Your Life

Paul the Apostle said it as well as it can be said. He understood it as well as it can be understood. He hit the nail on the head. *"The message of the cross is foolishness to those who are perishing, but to us who are being saved it is the power of God"* (1 Corinthians 1:18). Twenty centuries ago the God of the universe made a surprise attack on the forces of darkness. He did what hardly anyone was expecting. He came as a baby and died on a cross. We are badly mistaken if we think that was easy for first-century people to believe, but hard for people today. It was hard to believe then. It was hard for those closest to Jesus to believe. To many people it was downright foolishness. But to those who believed, to those who looked closely and decided there is good reason to believe, it was nothing less than the most powerful revelation ever received from the living God.

Nothing tells us more about life than this death. No event shows us more the character of God. No speech ever spoke so clearly about the values we all need. What happened when Jesus of Nazareth went to that hill outside the city gates will never in this world be fully understood. No scholar, preacher or poet can really take us to its depths. No one can fully fathom the mysteries that are here, but the closer we can get to it all, the better we will be. God wants a mighty movement in our day that will advance against darkness on every continent. But he will bless no movement that is not centered on the cross of Jesus Christ.

What we propose to do here is to spend thirty days thinking about the event that was like no other. I understand our unworthiness to come here, but I also know that the very nature of the cross allows us to do so. If, with the help of God, we do it well, these thirty days will lead to a lifetime of living with a new perspective and a greater appreciation for the power of God.

Plunging into these waters just makes us realize how deep they are. You will read what we have written and then perhaps see things that we have overlooked. My hope is that this exercise will inspire you to write your own book or at least encourage you to freely share with others what is written on your heart.

Those who have contributed to this work have one principal qualification: They believe in what they have written, and they live it. They have given up careers, possessions, comfortable surroundings and earthly security to be soldiers of the cross. They will all tell you that this was the best decision they have ever made. They have openly confessed their need for God and have humbled themselves before others in order to receive help and guidance. They are actively involved in helping other people to do the same.

This book is written primarily for those who have already embraced the cross and now seek to make it their "abiding place." Applications made each day will be made assuming that readers have been *"buried with Christ in baptism"* and *"united with him in his death"* (Romans 6:3, 5). But, if that has not happened, don't stop. Read on. What is shared here can help you, too, to understand why the cross is still the wisdom and the power of God.

—Tom A. Jones
Hermitage, Tennessee

PART I

Amazing Grace

Beneath the cross of Jesus
I fain would take my stand
. . .where heaven's love
and heaven's justice meet!

—Elizabeth Clephane

UNCONDITIONAL LOVE

While We Were Still Sinners

Tom A. Jones
Hermitage, Tennessee

We don't feel good at all when we know we are unloved. We don't feel much better when we aren't sure if we are loved. But what a difference it makes when we absolutely know that we are loved—when there has been a demonstration that proves it.

However, if we know we are loved because of our looks or our money or our performance, an insecurity lies just below the surface of those good feelings. As good as it feels to be loved, we know we could lose it if accident, illness, bankruptcy or failure were to rob us of those things that endear us to others.

When we stand at the foot of the cross and behold the love of God, we see how unbelievably unconditional his love is. You can lose your health, your possessions, even your reputation, and God's love for you will not be affected in the slightest. You can slip, sin or fail but if there were a seismograph that measured the smallest changes in love, the needle would not even quiver. While we were sinners—in the worst of shape—God demonstrated his love for us at the cross.

None of this is a testimony to God's softness on sin. No one—absolutely no one—is tougher on sin than God. It is, however, a testimony to how wide and long and high and deep the love of God is (Ephesians 3:18). It is a mystery of incredible proportions that God, who so hates sin, could so unconditionally love sinners. But this is what the cross demonstrates. This is what the cross makes clear. This is what the cross establishes, confirms and proves. There is a God; he is love; his love is unconditional. Nothing we can do or fail to do will stop him from loving us. It would be foolish to try to so antagonize God that he would stop loving you, but if you undertook that task, you would surely fail. He has already sent his Son to die for us while we were at our worst point. If we could look through to the core of God's character using some spiritual CAT scan or MRI, we would find unbelievably unconditional love, but no matter how sophisticated our technology might be, it would also fail us. It could never show the depth and breadth of this love *"that surpasses knowledge"* (Ephesians 3:19).

My wife and I and our three daughters taught a seminar together on instilling values in children. A few days after the seminar I began to think about the values we learn at the cross, about how God was communicating his most vital ones there at that point in time. Certainly, there is no higher value than unconditional love. Paul said there are faith, hope and love *"but the greatest of these is love"* (1 Corinthians 13:13).

We will be changed if we understand that no value characterizes God more than this one. A success doesn't cause God to love us a bit more. A failure doesn't cause him to love us a bit less. The cross proves it. Faith accepts it.

What does that mean for you today? If God loved you while you were his enemy, what does it mean now that you are his child? If he loved you last year when your work for him was flourishing, what does it mean now that you feel that dreaded "spiritual dryness"? What it means is wherever you are right now, whatever happened last year, last week or last night, God is for you. He is for you with the same passion he demonstrated at the cross. Our passions and enthusiasm wax and wane, but not God's. What he was then for you, he is now. The cross proves it. Faith accepts it.

Each time we stand at the foot of the cross, we should be more impressed with God. But there is more that needs to happen. We should be equally impressed that we are to be like him. *"Be imitators of God, therefore, as dearly loved children and live a life of love"* (Ephesians 5:1-2a). What I find in God at the cross, I need to put into my own heart and mind. The way God deals with me is the way I need to deal with others. There is only one place I need to go to learn how to treat my parents, my brothers and sisters, my wife, my children, my neighbors, strangers or my worst enemies—the cross. *"Dear friends, if God so loved us, we also ought to love one another"* (1 John 4:11). At the cross we learn what is right, and what is right is unconditional love. It was right for God to show it to us. It is right for us to show it to others. And how about this one: It is right for us to show it to God. Do you only love God when he performs like he should (i.e. in a way that pleases you)? Or do you love him unconditionally even as he loves you?

Is there anyone in your life right now that you love conditionally? Is there anyone you will care about only so long as they perform, look or treat you the way you think they should? Is there anyone you have stopped loving because they. . . ? (You finish the sentence.) Have you pulled back from God himself because he didn't give you an answer you wanted? A day at the foot of the cross calls us to ask such questions and to make changes in our own hearts.

Today, stand in awe of God. Look at the cross with wonder and amazement. Cry out with Paul, *"Christ Jesus came into the world to save sinners–of whom I am the worst"* (1 Timothy 1:15). Be astonished. Sing "amazing grace how sweet the sound." And then go love as you have been loved.

FOR FURTHER STUDY

Psalm 32

Matthew 18:23-35

Luke 15:11-32

John 3:16-18

Ephesians 2:1-10

HATING SIN

Feel the Pain

Randy McKean
Sterling, Virginia

> He himself bore our sins in his body on the tree, so that we might die to sins and live for righteousness; by his wounds you have been healed.
> —1 Peter 2:24

God made us in his image. We can feel pain because God feels pain. We can feel hurt because God feels hurt. When it comes to the cross—*feel the pain.* Understand that one of the most important truths of the cross is that sin—my sin and your sin—hurts God. This is the truth I must absolutely know and feel before I can be saved, but this is the same truth of which I must continually be more and more convicted to remain saved. When I look at the cross, I must see my sin and feel the pain—I must *feel God's pain.*

Question: Did you ever wholeheartedly love someone and then, they stopped loving you? Remember the pain? Now, feel God's pain!

Question: Have you ever had someone take advantage of you and use you? Remember the pain? Now, feel God's pain!

Question: Did you ever have a friend who turned on you? Remember the pain? Now, feel God's pain!

Question: Have you ever been neglected? Forgotten? Rejected? Betrayed? Remember the pain? Now, feel God's pain!

Amazing grace cost amazing pain. Feel God's pain—the pain endured because of our sin.

What would it feel like if the man or woman of your dreams committed his or her life to you in marriage and then was untrue to you—slept with another—committed adultery? How would you feel? Betrayed? Yes! Acutely hurt? Yes! Angry? Yes! Jealous? Yes! Deeply distressed? Yes! In fact, your world would seem to stop as your heart aches and breaks. This is how God feels when we are untrue to him—

when we "make love" with the world—when we commit spiritual adultery. Although our sins certainly hurt God before we totally commit our lives to him (it's like a marriage promise), I believe that our sins and unfaithfulness hurt God even more *after* our pledge to live for him. After all, this is how people feel about a relationship, and remember, we are made in the image of God.

> You adulterous people, don't you know that friendship with the world is hatred toward God? Anyone who chooses to be a friend of the world becomes an enemy of God. Or do you think Scripture says without reason that the spirit he caused to live in us envies intensely? (James 4:4-5).

How does God feel about a lack of care, a lack of trust? How does God feel about a sexual sin? How does God feel about being pushed aside for the sake of business or school? How does God feel about a lack of desire and excitement for him and about him? How would you feel about these things in a relationship? That's how God feels except so much more, because his love for us is so much more. The greater the capacity to love, the greater the capacity to feel pain. The greater the love, the greater the potential for being hurt. When it comes to the cross, it must state emphatically to us all the days of our lives—*feel the pain!*

Assume for a moment that you fall in love, get married and have the cutest baby in the world. (Your personal, unbiased opinion, of course!) One day your spouse is bringing groceries into the house, leaving the door open while your child plays on the floor. Suddenly, a large ferocious dog enters the house and grabs the child by the throat ripping the life out of the baby. You enter the room, see the pool of blood and your lifeless, disfigured child on the floor. The dog is crouched in the corner with blood drooling from its mouth. Now, what is your attitude towards the dog? Do you say, "Here doggy—you poor frightened thing?" Do you take your hand and comfort the dog by petting him? Of course not! You hate that dog. You want to destroy that dog because it just brutally killed the object of your love. In the same way, your sin put Jesus on the cross. Sin brutally murdered Jesus. So, how do you feel about your sin? Do you pet the sin? Do you go and play with the sin? Do you allow the sin to stay with you? No, you hate the sin. You want to destroy the sin because it murdered the object of your love. It killed your Jesus—your Savior.

Question: Honestly, how much do you hate sin? You will find that your hatred for sin is in proportion to your love for the one who died for you. The cross speaks of that love. Are

you emotionally in touch with your God? With your sin? With the cross?

I love my wife, Kay, and our children, Summer and Kent. I love being with them. I love playing with them. I love laughing with them. I love the easy, relaxing times. I love the hard, demanding times. I love the happy times. I love the tearful times. I love them. And because I love them, I don't want to hurt them. I don't want to do anything that might injure, interrupt, damage or sever those relationships. How much are you in love with God? How precious is that relationship to you? Sin hurts God. What's the depth of your desire not to hurt your God with your sin? In other words, how real is the cross for you?

Challenge: Today, make lasting decisions about your sin and your relationship with God.

How? It's really very simple—*feel the pain!*

> Submit yourselves, then, to God. Resist the devil, and he will flee from you. Come near to God and he will come near to you. Wash your hands, you sinners, and purify your hearts, you double-minded. Grieve, mourn and wail. Change your laughter to mourning and your joy to gloom. Humble yourselves before the Lord, and he will lift you up (James 4:7-10).

FOR FURTHER STUDY

Psalm 36

Isaiah 43:16-24, 53:4-6

Hosea 11

Luke 15:21-24

1 Corinthians 6:12-20

THE BLOOD
OF CHRIST

It Keeps On Cleansing

Marcia Lamb
Tewksbury, Massachusetts

The blood of Jesus, his Son, purifies us from all sin.

—1 John 1:7

It was a dark, starry night, and I was sitting on our front porch steps, crying. My tears were filled with grief, discouragement and self-disdain. As I rehashed my personal sins and failures over and over again, my spiritual barometer sank lower and lower. After a period of time, my husband, Roger, came out to see what was wrong. As I related my grievous list of sins and failures, he listened patiently and then encouraged me to repent, ask God for forgiveness and go on. "That's too easy!" I cried. How could such a wretched person as I get away with simply repenting. "Besides," I thought, "I'm weak; I'll probably sin again and again. Woe is me!"

Roger simply asked, "Are you trying to cry enough tears to earn your forgiveness?" The absurdity of the thought brought me to my senses. Obviously, there was no way that I could cry enough tears to gain forgiveness. What could I do to equal what Jesus had already done for me? Could I do enough good deeds, stay perfectly pure, crawl on my knees far enough, give enough money, pray loudly enough or convert enough sinners? Nothing I could do could come close to his sacrifice of love and grace.

The truth suddenly became very clear. Jesus' shed blood was the only thing that could possibly attain forgiveness for me (Ephesians 1:7).

By revisiting the cross in my thoughts on a daily basis, I began to have more faith in his blood as a continual cleansing agent. It was not meant to be a once-in-a-lifetime event. Romans 5:9 reminds us that *"since we have now been justified by his blood, how much more shall we be saved from God's wrath through him!"* The benefits of his blood are assured to us as his children. Shed blood has always been a significant part of God's covenant of forgiveness. Leviticus 17:11 says, *"For the life of a creature is in the blood, and I have given it to you to make atonement for yourselves on the altar; it is the blood that makes atonement for one's life."* Shed blood represents one life given for another. In the NIV *Application Bible*, there is a helpful footnote on this verse:

> How does blood make atonement for sin? On the one hand, blood represents the sinner's life infected by his sin and headed for death. On the other hand the blood represents the innocent life of the animal that was sacrificed in place of the guilty person making the offering. The death of the animal (of which blood was the proof) fulfilled the penalty of death. God therefore granted forgiveness to the sinner. It is God who forgives based on the faith of the person doing the sacrificing.

Our thinking that God's plan for forgiveness is too easy, too hard or somehow faulty is as absurd as an Israelite struggling with offering his sacrificial lamb. We can imagine the poor priest trying to persuade the Israelite to trust God's ways and offer the lamb. The worshipper could have tried to substitute a bucket of tears, 365 good deeds a year, or weeks of prayer and fasting. He could also pridefully have tried to reach enough perfection to crawl up on the altar himself to spare the innocent lamb. Do we have more faith in our weak, self-invented sacrifices than we do in God's perfect plan of grace? Jesus' sacrifice for our sins must be accepted first, then our joyful sacrificial life for God makes sense.

Years later when I developed life-threatening cancer, I was made grateful for that earlier understanding of God's blood-bought grace. Suddenly, I could not "produce" as many good deeds and generally do as much in the Kingdom as before. Doubts and fears flooded my mind. Would these meager efforts be good enough for God? Was I being punished for unresolved sin? The deeper I dug for answers, the simpler and more profound the answer came back, *"God so loved the world that he gave his one and only Son"* (John 3:16).

Wasn't Christ's suffering and death enough proof of God's willingness to love and forgive? The second part of John 3:16 rang in my ears too, *"that whoever believes in him shall not perish but have eternal life."* Again my faith in God and his plan was the real issue. Would I accept my value and worth based on being a blood-bought sinner and not on my ability to produce a perfect life?

As young Christians we often understand our initial forgiveness through Christ's shed blood, but later on we may fail to appreciate how it continues to save us. We need to realize that we are in Christ continually receiving the benefits of his blood (Galatians 3:26). 1 John 1:7 explains that *"if we walk in the light, as he is in the light. . .the blood of Jesus, his Son, purifies us from all sin."* The word "purifies" is in the continual present tense (i.e. "it keeps on cleansing"). This means a day-by-day, constant cleansing.

I can relate this to the cancerous blood cells that were attacking our son Michael's body when he had leukemia at age six. The enemy was destroyed and removed by chemotherapy so that the natural healing power of his blood could continue to do its work. Realizing that blood provides food, oxygen, cleansing, healing and defense against germs, we can see how the spiritual cleansing work of Christ's blood can continually and effectively maintain our forgiveness. His blood is keeping us "cured" as we openly confess, repent and appeal to God for forgiveness (1 John 1:8-2:6).

With greater understanding and faith in the cleansing power of Jesus' blood, what will you do the next time you are convicted of sin? Will you pull out your old, useless, self-invented sacrifices, or will you appeal to God's grace through Christ's continual atoning blood? Will you wallow in self-pity, or will you celebrate Jesus' ongoing work in your behalf?

Editors' note: both Michael and Marcia fully recovered from their cancers.

FOR FURTHER STUDY

Psalm 130

Romans 5:1-11

Hebrews 9:15-22

1 Peter 1:18-20

1 John 1:5-10

FORGIVENESS

The Freedom of Forgiveness

Theresa Ferguson
McKinney, Texas

> Be kind and compassionate to one another, forgiving each other, just as in Christ God forgave you.
>
> Be imitators of God, therefore, as dearly loved children and live a life of love, just as Christ loved us and gave himself up for us as a fragrant offering and sacrifice to God.
>
> —Ephesians 4:32-5:2

True forgiveness from the heart is not a normal human virtue—it is clearly a divine virtue made possible by God. The motivation for forgiveness is provided in the cross of our Lord, who loved us and sacrificed himself for us. His life demonstrated a type of forgiveness that truly amazes us in its consistency and completeness. As we imitate his life, then and only then will we be able to forgive one another from the heart. What enabled him to live out so fully this most challenging quality?

For one thing, he faced the truth. *He faced the truth* of just how unfair and cruel life could be in a physical sense. Living a totally sinless life and pouring out that life for everyone except himself should have won everyone over to God. Instead, it "won" rejection and hatred! That doesn't seem fair, does it? Unlike you and me, Jesus did not expect life to be fair—he simply expected God to be fair. Further, his view of God's fairness was not tainted by selfishness. He accepted everything from the hand of God virtually without question. That is amazing! Never did he try to deal with such emotional issues by putting them out of his mind—by "stuffing" them. Nor did he allow the way he was treated to affect the loving way that he treated others.

Even Judas, his known betrayer, received only kindness from him.

Jesus knew that he must not only demonstrate forgiveness—he must carefully train his disciples to practice it. In the parable of the unmerciful servant (Matthew 18:21-35), he was teaching the absolute necessity of unlimited forgiveness from the heart. In Luke 17:1-5, he taught the disciples to forgive the same brother seven times in one day. No wonder they begged for increased faith!

He not only faced the truth—*he also felt the pain*. He was completely in touch intellectually and emotionally with the harsh realities of his life. Jesus was not afraid to be totally honest with his feelings, both before God and before man. Acting as if the hurt didn't really happen, or didn't hurt *much,* is not the Christlike path of forgiveness. Perhaps the greatest pain Jesus felt emotionally was experienced in the Garden of Gethsemane. There, he felt enough pain to cause him to sweat blood. He may have been anticipating a spiritual separation from the Father as he bore the sins of the whole world. When that anticipation became reality, he screamed out in deep anguish, *"My God, my God, why have you forsaken me?"* His commitment to forgiveness was based on an acceptance of every pain possible—physical, spiritual and emotional.

Finally, Jesus *freed his heart* in order to accomplish the ultimate in forgiveness. Freeing his heart, in a word, meant trust. He trusted his Father and focused on him rather than on his own pain. He responded in prayer at the most difficult times in his life. In the garden, after pleading for a removal of the cup, he prayed for God's will to be done instead of his own. On the cross, he prayed for the forgiveness of his enemies. He yielded to God's sense of justice in what seemed to be the most unjust situation in the world. In the words of Peter, *"When they hurled their insults at him, he did not retaliate; when he suffered, he made no threats. Instead, he entrusted himself to him who judges justly"* (1 Peter 2:23). He surrendered his life to God as he said from the cross, *"Father, into your hands I commit my spirit"* (Luke 23:46). In spite of all the pain and rejection and suffering, he faced death without any trace of bitterness toward God or man. Therefore, his trust was rewarded with a resurrection of victory over the sins of the world, and forgiveness was assured!

As we begin to imitate Jesus' example of forgiveness, we also must face the truth, feel the pain, and free our hearts. In dealing with my own hurts, whether from my distant past or recent past, I have had to get honest about the realities of my life. I have had to call sin, sin, whether it be others' sin toward me or my own sin in response to pain caused by others. Truth, no matter how painful, must be faced and dealt with by the power of God. It cannot be denied or watered down. At times it is tempting to rationalize away our sins or the sins of those we love. But forgiveness cannot be attained until everything has been brought out into the light, and the sooner, the better.

Seeing the truth of our hurts must be followed by allowing ourselves to feel the pain incurred. Most likely, these feelings will produce a reaction of either fear or anger or both. These reactions must be worked through and surrendered to God, or else they will lead to bitterness, resentment, rage, malice or apathy. (See Ephesians 4:31.) If we do not deal with our damaged emotions and put our anger to rest, we will forever keep a record of wrongs, making our own selves miserable and ruling out our own forgiveness which God is eager to grant (Matthew 6:14-15).

Once we face reality and feel reality, then we are able to have our hearts set free by the grace of a forgiving God. It requires of us, as it did of Jesus, a complete trust in God's providence, believing he is really in control of our lives and definitely wants the very best for us. We must accept these facts, refuse to let self-focused emotions rob us of surrender, and take responsibility for our sinful reactions to being sinned against. If someone needs to be disciplined for causing you pain, leave it all up to God (Romans 12:19). Make a firm decision to forgive, and refuse to let anything or anyone stop you from carrying out that decision. When you have truly replaced the evil with good, you will know it, for then your very soul will be flooded with a peace which transcends all understanding (Philippians 4:7).

FOR FURTHER STUDY

Hosea 14:1-2
Matthew 18:21-35
Luke 17:1-4
Ephesians 4:31-32
1 Peter 2:18-25

BAPTISM

Back to the Future

Roger Lamb
Tewksbury, Massachusetts

> Or don't you know that all of us who were baptized into Christ Jesus were baptized into his death? We were therefore buried with him through baptism into death in order that, just as Christ was raised from the dead through the glory of the Father, we too may live a new life.
>
> —Romans 6:3-4

To a person living 2,000 years after Jesus was on earth, the cross seems a remote experience. In the day of CNN worldwide instant information overload, last hour's headline news is obsolete. If I can't even relate to yesterday, how can I personally buy into an event in ancient history?

Often our best questions are great opportunities for the display of God's clever designs. History is just the backdrop for his skillful hand to creatively and passionately portray his grand plan for man. This is never more true than in his plan to forever connect every willing man and woman by baptism to the focal point of human history, the cross of his only Son.

The apostle Paul, writing the words above about twenty years after his own baptism, seems astonished as he recounts for the Christians in Rome their link to the cross. God did not just intend for Jesus to experience the cross, but for each one of us to know that incredible moment of dying to self and to a sinful world and being raised to a new life as unselfish conquerors. In every age all who have personally committed to be disciples of Jesus, tasted the bittersweetness of repentance, and in baptism felt the closing coffin of water over their faces have known the exhilarating joy of bursting out of the grave with a new heart and a new lease on life.

This is no mystical feat in need of a test tube, a spell or a mantra. In baptism you were *"buried with him...and raised with him through your faith in the power of God, who raised him from the dead"* (Colossians 2:12). There is more power in authentic faith than in any science, witch doctor or guru.

It's no accident either. On the inauguration day of the church in Acts 2, Peter knew then that the cross he had witnessed as a coward was the connecting point for every human being to God, no matter what their address or century. *"Repent and be baptized, everyone of you, in the name of Jesus Christ so that your sins may be forgiven. And you will receive the gift of the Holy Spirit. The promise is for you and your children and for all who are far off—for all whom the Lord our God will call"* (Acts 2:38-39). Seven years later God opened Peter's eyes to see that all along this also meant for every race.

Are you still far off? Or are you connected? If you have been baptized into his death and raised out of your own spiritual tomb, you know. Death and resurrection are hard things to forget. Now walk in the confidence of a man or woman who has been to the cross and walked out of the tomb. *"For we know that our old self was crucified with him so that the body of sin might be rendered powerless, that we should no longer be slaves to sin—because anyone who has died has been freed from sin"* (Romans 6:6-7).

Today take a trip back to the cross and the empty tomb of Jesus. Stop by your own cross and empty watery tomb. Remember all the sins that controlled you before baptism. Remember the guilt and the pain you left there. Remember the first breath of air as you were born again and the indescribable joy of your new family. For a moment recall your first infant words to your Father in prayer. Then visit the crosses and empty tombs of your best friends in the Kingdom, and wind up pausing at the sites of those you helped to become disciples. These are the most exciting and fulfilling sites. With them you saw and understood the whole scene much better than with your own. You were able to love them through their decisions to take up their crosses and follow Jesus. You were by each one's side as they died to their old life, and you felt like a midwife when they were born again.

A number of years ago, our oldest son, Michael, while studying the Bible with his teen ministry leader, had been making obvious changes in his attitudes and behavior. Early one summer evening he asked Marcia and me if we could talk. After directing us to the couch in the living room, he curiously disappeared. Soon this strapping, handsome teenager with the broad shoulders reappeared with a bowl of water and a towel. Tearfully, as he washed our feet, he shared his sins with us, asked for forgiveness and told us he wanted to become a disciple. As I baptized him I couldn't help but think about the numerous prayers said for his being cured of leukemia. This was even better that that.

As David, our youngest, was studying the Bible to become a Christian, he and I shared an incredible Saturday afternoon on our porch. For the first time in his life he was struggling with his separation from God. We both wept as he confessed sins I knew nothing about, and the next day we both laughed and celebrated as I brought him up out of his sin-grave at baptism.

Marcia and I often think of Christie's baptism now that she is living in an apartment with other disciples. We don't share the fears of our community friends who have daughters away from home. Instead of worrying about where she is, what she is doing and when we are going to have a conversation about her needing an abortion or an AIDS test, our greatest concern is when we will get to meet the next person she brings to the Lord.

Now turn your sights on the crosses that are still empty. There's a name on each one. But each person has to decide to pick up his or her own. No one can do it for him or her, but you can call them to it. Family, friends and even people you've not yet encountered can all come to Jesus' cross today.

FOR FURTHER STUDY

2 Kings 5:1-14

Galatians 3:26-29

Colossians 2:9-15

1 Peter 3:18-22

Always Remembering

Chelly Larson
Eden Prairie, Minnesota

When the hour came, Jesus and his apostles reclined at the table. And he said to them, "I have eagerly desired to eat this Passover with you before I suffer."

. . . And he took bread, gave thanks and broke it, and gave it to them, saying, "This is my body given for you; do this in remembrance of me."

In the same way, after the supper he took the cup, saying, "This cup is the new covenant in my blood, which is poured out for you."

—Luke 22:14-15, 19-20

Passover. To the Jews the word pulsed with freedom. This was a special time to remember the deliverance of the people of Israel from their slavery in Egypt (Exodus 12). On the night that the Israelites were freed, the Lord struck down the first-born son of every Egyptian family. He passed over the homes of the Israelites because the blood of a sacrificed lamb was smeared on the doorframe to set them apart. On that night they left so quickly that they did not have time to bake bread with leaven, so it was unleavened bread that they ate.

By the time of the first century, thousands of people gathered in Jerusalem each year to celebrate this feast of great meaning. During the Passover all lodging was free, and it was very common for a rabbi to use an upper room to meet with his disciples to share his heart. It was in just such an upper room that Jesus celebrated this feast with his disciples, and in so doing, gave it new meaning. Jesus chose the Passover as the time he would come to Jerusalem to die—to be the sacrificial lamb whose blood would be smeared over the lives of his followers. He came to die so that they might be set free.

Jesus said, *"This cup is the new covenant in my blood."* The new covenant—the new relationship between man and God that his sacrifice would make possible. He spoke of a divinely initiated reconciliation. Mankind was the object of God's affection, the apple of his eye. But man had hurt God with his sin and had separated himself from his Creator.

But now the new covenant, the new plan, the perfect, once-for-all sacrifice had come, replacing a Jewish sacrificial system that could only look forward to such atonement ("at onement"). It was at the last supper that Jesus revealed the message of hope, the solution, the reason he came. In essence Jesus said, "With my life and death I am making it possible for you to have a new relationship with God. Now remember this!" As momentous as his sacrifice was, it would be forgotten if plans were not made to remember.

We are just like the Twelve. In the midst of the activities and pressure of life, we, too, forget the incredible love our Lord has for us. We forget the Bread of Life. We forget how much he went through for us to be united with God. We forget that we can be forgiven and start over again and again, and that we do have the power to change because of the power of the cross. We forget why we are doing the things we are doing. Our Lord knew that in order for us to maintain motivation and focus we would need to come together and go to the foot of the cross to remember.

"And he took bread, gave thanks and broke it" (Luke 22:19). Jesus, about to die, gave thanks. Jesus, about to be separated from God, gave thanks. Why? Because the Father's will was going to be accomplished and people's lives would be changed.

This Sunday as you stand at the cross, cry out in your heart, "And what can separate us from the love of Christ?" and give thanks. No matter what happened this week, give thanks. It was for you that he died. He was tied so that you could be set free. He was separated from God so that you would never have to be again.

But as you give thanks, examine yourself (1 Corinthians 11:28). Envision the cross, humble your heart and let it reveal sin that needs to be confessed and crucified. In view of the cross, how could you hold on to it one more moment? Self-examination is different from self-condemnation. As we honestly take stock of our hearts, attitudes, motives and actions, we should be driven to the blood of Christ for forgiveness. There is no need for ongoing guilt or worldly sorrow. For even our tears of repentance must be washed in the blood of Christ.

As we examine ourselves we need to remember our identity in Christ and remember that there is no more condemnation for us (Romans 8:1). We have received the most incredible gift of all—we have been set free from our bondage to sin.

God not only forgives our sin, he cleanses our consciences completely. He threw our sins deep into the ocean and, in the words of Corrie ten Boom (*Each New Day*, Revell, 1977), he has posted a "NO FISHING" sign on the shore.

Sometime ago I read a story about a soldier who wanted to meet the woman whose blood donation had saved his life. A time and place was arranged, and in a moving scene, the grateful soldier recounted his ordeal to his life-saving benefactor. They both wept with thankfulness.

How much more do we need to weep in thanksgiving for the most precious blood donor of all? Are you remembering the Lord as he asked? During the supper every Sunday are you grateful for his sacrifice? Does this special time pulse with freedom for you?

FOR FURTHER STUDY

Exodus 12

Isaiah 53

Romans 8:31-39, 12:1-2

1 Corinthians 11:17-34

WISDOM

The Wisdom and the Power of God

Roy Larson
Eden Prairie, Minnesota

For the message of the cross is foolishness to those who are perishing, but to us who are being saved it is the power of God.
—1 Corinthians 1:18

Will the cross ever make sense to the world? Don't hold your breath waiting for it to happen. For centuries the message of the cross has been *"a stumbling block to Jews and foolishness to Gentiles, but to those whom God has called...Christ the power of God and the wisdom of God"* (1 Corinthians 1:23-24). In the cross we see the ultimate display of God's wisdom and power, the fulfillment of his eternal plan for man's redemption. But what he did has been misunderstood for centuries.

In 1 Corinthians 1:19 Paul quoted Isaiah to show how human wisdom is bound to fail. With all its wisdom, the world had never found God. This search was destined to frustration by God himself to show men their helplessness and prepare the way for the acceptance of Christ.

The message of the cross was a great stumbling block to Jews because they could not believe someone hung on a cross could be the Messiah. Didn't their Scriptures say it? *"Anyone who is hung on a tree is under God's curse"* (Deuteronomy 21:23). They overlooked the detailed description of the suffering Messiah in Isaiah 53 and sought instead a miracle-working general to lead them with swords against the Romans. The innocent and humble man willing to suffer for the sins of others did not impress them.

The message of the cross was foolishness to Greeks because for them God was described with the word *apatheia*—a total inability to feel. Therefore, if God could experience emotions like grief or sorrow then some man could influence God and therefore be greater than God. A suffering God was an impossible concept for the sophisticated Greek thinker to accept. The Greeks admired men with clever minds and silver tongues. The philosophers would sit around and spend hours splitting hairs and debating subjects (Acts 17:18-21). Intoxicated with their knowledge and fine words, they found the Christian message blunt and crude. They laughed at and looked down on the messengers of Christ as uncultured and unsophisticated men. In 1 Corinthians 4:10-13, Paul said, *"We are fools for Christ...we have become the scum of the earth, the refuse of the world."*

Quite obviously God's plan was never to impress prideful scholars or find acceptance among the philosophers or rulers of this age, but to rock this planet with what it needed most—the truth. Choosing the weak and lowly things, he shamed the strong and influential so no one could boast before him. He took a despised cross and a mocked, abused man on it and brought something the world could never produce—righteousness, holiness and redemption (1 Cor. 1:26-31).

Some things never change. Today the spirit of the Jews and Greeks lives on. The message of the cross is no more acceptable now than it was then. Even among the religious community, denying self and taking up the cross is seen as crude. Something much kinder, gentler and less judgmental is preferred. The wisdom of God gives way to the latest psychological terms and ideas, and man once again shows his confidence in his ability (and at the same time reveals his arrogance).

Some of the top minds in our world will look at those who preach the cross and call others to it and see dangerous fanatics. Curiously, the same person will look at a graduate student who spends 80-100 hours a week in the laboratory and praise his or her dedication. An athlete who trains daily for six to eight hours will be applauded for competitive spirit and commitment. A young executive who puts in 60 hours a week in the office will be praised for devotion to the company. But let someone be just as passionate for the cross of Christ, and the criticism will come in waves.

The world praises secular devotion with positive words like "devoted," "committed" and "excellent." However, these same lips can smear the disciple of Christ devoted to the cause of Christ with a host of negative, destructive terms. The message of the cross is foolishness to those who are perishing.

"The man without the Spirit does not accept the things that come from the Spirit of God, for they are foolishness to him, and he cannot understand them" (1 Corinthians 2:14).

"The god of this age has blinded the minds of unbelievers, so that they cannot see the light of the gospel of the glory of Christ, who is the image of God" (2 Corinthians 4:4).

The wise of this world, blinded by their arrogance and pride, simply cannot see how powerfully the cross is changing lives, changing marriages, changing families, and changing racial and ethnic relations. They cannot see how the cross is teaching people how to forgive, how to change and how to love.

We simply need to accept that we will never be accepted by the religious community, the intellectual world or the popular media. The message of the cross always has been and will be foolishness to those who are perishing.

God didn't come to impress the world. How about you? Do you have deep convictions that will never erode with the crashing waves of persecution and secular intellectual arguments? Are you ready to take the wisdom and power of God and *"demolish arguments and every pretension that sets itself up against the knowledge of God"* (2 Corinthians 10:5)?

God's wisdom and man's wisdom are far different. Be sure you never confuse them. While the world viewed the cross as the ultimate failure and disgrace, all of Heaven praised God for Christ and his cross—the wisdom and power of God!

FOR FURTHER STUDY

Isaiah 55:8-11

1 Corinthians 1-3, 4:18-21

2 Corinthians 10:1-5

James 3:13-18

BOASTING

Who Gets the Credit?

Sheila Jones
Hermitage, Tennessee

> May I never boast except in the cross of our Lord Jesus Christ, through which the world has been crucified to me, and I to the world.
>
> —Galatians 6:14

"I did it all by myself." The boast of a two-year-old who has just put his shoes on for the first time? No, the thought of a thirty-two-year-old who has just completed the marathon. Or of a twenty-seven-year-old who has just received the Employee of the Month Award. How quick human nature is to accept credit for certain accomplishments. How quick human nature is to forget that God made us and enables us to run, to think, to breathe. Paul asks us, *"What do you have that you did not receive? And if you did receive it, why do you boast as if you did not?"* (1 Corinthians 4:7b).

We like to feel strong, to feel adequate, to feel talented. It builds our self-esteem. It verifies our worth. And so we look for reasons to boast. Of course, we often don't recognize it as boasting. We don't see the arrogance in our hearts as we self-sufficiently go into our day without prayer. We are, in effect, saying, *"I can do it all by myself." We are saying, "Today...[I] will go to this or that city"* (James 4:13). James says we are boasting and bragging.

Do we think that Paul had low self-esteem because he said, *"I will not boast about myself, except about my weaknesses"* (2 Corinthians 12:5b)? Does low self-esteem motivate someone to be the selfless, compassionate, pivotal leader of a persecuted, fledgling movement? Boast in our weaknesses? It is upside down. It is inside out. And, yet, it is true—through and through. Paul's commitment was clear. "May I never boast except in the cross of our Lord Jesus Christ." The cross affirms our worth. The cross frees us from performing, from making sure we get the credit due us. In our old nature, we take that credit and very carefully wrap our sense of worth around it. We are fearful of losing any credit, because that would lessen the amount of worth that we could wrap around it. Less credit—less worth, we reason.

Why was Paul willing to boast about his weaknesses? He lets us in on the secret: "I will boast all the more gladly about my weaknesses, so that Christ's power may rest on me....For when I am weak, then I am strong" (2 Corinthians 12:9b, 10b). Who wouldn't want the power of God in his life? The power that created a universe out of nothing. The power that parted the Red Sea. The power that raised a very dead man from the grave never to die again. Who wouldn't want it? But how does Paul say you can have that power? By boasting in your weaknesses. By not making sure you get credit for all your strengths. Upside down. Inside out. But true—through and through.

So, how do we respond to this? Do we snivel around saying, "I'm so weak. I can't do anything. I'm no good to anybody"? Remember what Paul said, "When I am weak, then I am strong." The person who truly boasts in the cross and in what Jesus has done for her is a strong person. A person who does not rely on recognition from others to stay faithful to God. A person who does not pull away from others if they do not seem to appreciate her enough. Yes, a strong person. A person who can take correction without having to prove all the ways she is right. A person who is secure enough in her own worth that she can tell the truth to someone who might reject her. A person who does not have to prove she already knew something before she was told. Bottom line: a person who can admit her inadequacies and confess her sins and look to God for verification. One who is free of the need to project an image or prove her worth. And one through whom the power of God is able to flow unhindered. Such a person is not boastful, but is humble. Such a person is strong, spiritual and puts her trust in God. Are you such a person? Do you want to be such a person?

In my old nature I look to be affirmed, to be given credit for all that I do. I naturally try to prove that I am worthy of others' love and respect. A competitive spirit, a self-oozing instead of self-losing spirit spits out of my heart apart from Jesus. At times, I have been publicly affirmed for something I really did not do. Certain traits were ascribed to me that I personally did not see. On the other hand, my name has also been left out of the "list of credits" for things I played a major role in accomplishing. A little voice comes up in me that wants to set the record straight on both counts. But the cross says that the record has already been set straight. All credit to Jesus. So be it.

Thanks be to God that Jesus has taken the "credit" for my prideful heart and that he has given me credit for his righteousness. The reckoning miracle of the cross. Therefore, all credit for my own righteousness is his.

As you look at your own heart, are you boastful or are you humble? Do you trust in yourself and your own abilities, or do you trust in God? Do you acknowledge that your talents are gifts from God, or do you feel better than others in the areas of your strengths? Are you trying to earn your salvation, or are you grateful that Jesus has already won it? Do you push others away in your need to prove yourself, or do you draw others to you through your vulnerability?

Boast in your weaknesses. Live in the power of God. It is upside down. It is inside out. But it is true—through and through.

FOR FURTHER STUDY

Deuteronomy 8:10-18

Daniel 4:28-37

Romans 4

1 Corinthians 2:1-5

PART II

"Follow Me"

Were the whole realm of
nature mine, that were a
present far too small.

Love so amazing, so divine
demands my soul, my life
my all.

—Isaac Watts

SURRENDER

Life Through Death

Gordon Ferguson
McKinney, Texas

Jesus replied, "The hour has come for the Son of Man to be glorified. I tell you the truth, unless a kernel of wheat falls to the ground and dies, it remains only a single seed. But if it dies, it produces many seeds. The man who loves his life will lose it, while the man who hates his life in this world will keep it for eternal life."

—John 12:23-25

Ironically, one of the greatest evidences of the inspiration of the Scriptures is seen in the paradoxes they contain. God's wisdom is absolutely opposite to the normal thinking processes of men. Victory comes through surrender. Strength comes through weakness. Life comes through death. Such concepts are not difficult to accept intellectually if we are followers of Christ. But internalizing these concepts into our hearts so that they permeate our thinking and doing is another matter indeed.

Denying self and taking up a cross daily is very difficult. Voluntary surrender is not easy. Crosses are neither comfortable nor enjoyable. But the path to Golgotha remains the only way home. Christ cannot be formed in us until we are crucified with him (Galatians 2:20, 4:19).

Jesus came to give life by freeing us from bondage. The difficulty in gaining freedom is that the bondage is far deeper than we usually imagine. Specific sins are not so much the issue. What is more important is the root of sin. Rebellion against God and his law is brought about by man's desire to *be* God. Adam and Eve wanted to be like God and to stand in his place. The desire to control is ingrained in us deeply. We become adept manipulators of people and circumstances and are bold enough to try the same even with God. Selfishness is an incredibly pervasive sin!

Jesus came to free us from this dreadful malady. Satan, however, works to dilute the solution into a substitute which will not satisfy. In essence, he dupes us into exchanging the bondage of sin for the bondage of powerless religion. And we are fairly easy to fool because God's way looks too painful. Therefore, we often avoid the cross and remain alive to our self-promoting tendencies. We may appear spiritual and act spiritual, but still be controlled by the old self.

When this phenomenon occurs, our lives do not change at the deepest level, and we continue to struggle with much the same problems that the world does. If this failure continues for long enough, we are strongly tempted to go back into the world. Some who take this route then claim to be happier. While I once would have argued with their claim, I now do not. They are happier. The only burden which is heavier than that of sin is the yoke of a powerless religion. Attempting to practice a self-propelled Christianity cannot satisfy the soul's deepest needs, nor can it last indefinitely.

The whole Bible is designed to help us see our sad lack of goodness and power. Only when we are sick of our old nature will we be convinced sufficiently to totally sell out to God. At that point, we are willing to face even the cross. Death to self seems preferable to life. We then are ready to crucify pride and selfishness through surrender.

Most of our crises are designed to produce our surrender and the subsequent growth it brings. Even Jesus was perfected for his task of serving through suffering (Hebrews 5:8-9). We need not imagine that we will be matured without it (Hebrews 12:5-11, James 1:2-3). It is through many hardships that we enter the heavenly kingdom (Acts 14:22). And many of these hardships come about because we refuse to stay surrendered, and thus we must once again be taught the futility of self-reliance. If we are hard-headed and hard-hearted, we may renew our efforts to pull ourselves up by our own bootstraps. In this case, most of our solutions only prolong the battle and block our way to freedom.

We human beings are our own worst enemies. We want control.

We want our own judgment, our opinions, our desires, our power! We refuse to deny self daily and stay surrendered. Therefore, failure and frustration creep in once more. Much of this frustration and anger is actually directed at God, even though we may not realize it. We may blame him for not answering our prayers in the way we think he should. Truthfully, our prayers are often little more than requests for God to rubber-stamp our selfish desires. We commonly have far more self in our religion than we think.

Surrender, or death to self, is an emotional break with self being in control. We become willing to yield our lives, our health, our family, our finances, our future and our plans totally to him. We are willing to accept what we need rather than stubbornly to insist on what we want. In essence, we allow God to be God in our daily lives. Amazingly, real life follows as a great calmness pervades our entire being, otherwise known as the *"peace which passes understanding"* (Philippians 4:7). True meaning and purpose come into focus, and productivity begins. Crucifixion gives way to resurrection!

Even if we grasp the concept of surrender on an intellectual level, we may have a much more difficult time with the emotional release to God. All of us struggle with *staying* surrendered on a sustained basis. Just how do we go about taking up a cross of self-denial daily?

First, be absolutely committed to the concept. Any doubts or reservations will keep you from surrendering. Read John 12:23-25; Luke 9:23-24, 14:25-33. Either we are the lord of our lives or God is, for there can be no in-between. Sell out or you will end up getting out!

Second, be committed to prayer about surrender. Pray about your decision to surrender. Ask God to help you surrender. Be willing to be made willing. Since faith, surrender and trust are much the same, pray, "I surrender; help my lack of surrender." Pray about all of the specific ways in which you need to surrender.

Third, be committed to a relationship with another disciple. Share your convictions and your plans. Keep open about your struggles with being surrendered. Ask for help and pray together about it.

Fourth, be committed to stretching your comfort zone. Do things for God that you know you cannot do without his help. Never pass up an opportunity to serve. Do not be stopped by fears, for they can easily produce cowardice rather than surrender. Read 1 Corinthians 2:1-5 and 2 Corinthians 12:7-10.

Finally, realize that surrender brings about absolute freedom. With God in control, you can relax and enjoy life, living in his strength. Let go and let God, and *life through death* will cease to be a puzzling paradox!

FOR FURTHER STUDY

Isaiah 42:5-7

Matthew 26:36-46

Colossians 1:13-14, 2:8

2 Timothy 2:25-26

James 4:1-3

Denial Without Regret

Javier Amayz
Boston, Massachusetts

> Jesus Christ laid down his life for us. And we ought to lay down our lives for our brothers.
>
> 1 John 3:16

And Jesus said, "That's enough!...Have him do it, not me!... That's not my responsibility!...I'm tired; let somebody else do it... .I'll do it later!...Why me?...You do it...It's too late, and I've done enough...That's not my job...Get off my back!...I'll do it at my pace and when I feel like it."

Jesus had plenty of opportunities to say such things, but he never did. Even as they took him to a cross, he uttered no such words. In situation after situation, the Son of God denied himself and was faithful to his Father and his calling.

What is self-denial if not the decision to consistently lay down our lives. Not a popular topic in business seminars, self-development symposia or the like, the denial of self is at the heart of following Jesus. No one can follow Jesus far without seeing his conviction about denying himself and hearing his challenge for us to do the same.

Jesus' struggle in Gethsemane shows us that the battle to deny self must be fought and won in prayer (Matthew 26:36-46). Though he loved God with all his heart, he went to that place with his will and the Father's being separate. The cup God set before him was one he did not want to take. Yet, through agonizing prayer, meditation and more prayer, he gave up what he wanted and united his will with God's. Without self-denial there would have been no cross. Without the cross there would have been no salvation. Our very souls depended on his saying "no" to self.

The very next day, this time bleeding as he hung on the tree, Jesus taught us again a lesson in denying self. Surely tempted to focus on his own pain, he forgave his tormentors (Luke 23:34), ministered to a criminal (Luke 23:43), and provided for his mother (John 19:27). Jesus set an unblemished example of this hard teaching of self-denial. He was convinced it was right and that God would bless it. Let us be inspired by his example and compelled to imitate him!

"If anyone would come after me, he must deny himself" (Luke 9:23).

When introduced to Jesus Christ, we are attracted by his love, his inspiration and his care for others. He calls us to imitate him, and that is exciting. But there is no way to love and serve others as Jesus did and avoid denying ourselves. Any limitation we put on self-denial will surely limit our usefulness to him and the way God can bless us.

There are times when self-denial comes relatively naturally. My wife and I have two daughters and are guardians of my brother-in-law. It is relatively easy to stay up and care for these special family members when they are sick and in need of our attention. But when it comes to denying self for strangers, that's love in a whole different realm. But Jesus has sent us out to love strangers and even enemies. This doesn't mean to offer them a few crumbs but to offer them our very selves.

Regardless of where you live in the world, there are needs all around you. Just open your eyes, and you can find many opportunities to help, to serve and to transform someone else's life. It is clearly God's will that you see the needs and meet them (Matthew 25:31-46). If your tendency is to think "Why should I?" just remember (1) you are a disciple, (2) it is right and (3) God will bless it.

A day of self-denial must begin with a morning of preparation. Surely Jesus was able to wash the feet of others at the end of a day because at the beginning of it, he was preparing his mind through communion with God. Decide early in every day that you will not be too busy to notice others or so consumed with your life that you will not be available to help another. As you walk out the door of your house, pray for help in forgetting yourself and in seeing and meeting the needs of others.

As you grow in your level of self denial, remember the old saying about the cobbler's children having no shoes. The world may know you as one who is the helper of all, but how are you known at home? Do you work on self-denial from 9 to 5 only to promptly forget about it when you walk into the house? Make it your life! Transform it into a character trait. Battle for it, and restore it constantly through prayer, study and decision. Decide never to turn that doorknob until you are ready to go in and be a giver rather than a taker.

As life-situations change, so do our opportunities to deny ourselves. As we get a new roommate or a new spouse, new children or even a new disciple, character-revealing challenges are provided. How do you see them? As burdens or as opportunities to give of yourself in new ways?

Jesus laid down his life again and again and again until there was nothing left to give. But he never resented it or regretted it, because the seed that falls to the ground and dies does produce much fruit.

Let us go to the cross...and deny ourselves...again and again and again, until there is nothing left to give.

FOR FURTHER STUDY

Romans 5:1-11

Philippians 2:1-11

James 2:14-26

1 John 3:11-20

To Heights of Humility

Tom Franz
Minneapolis, Minnesota

Your attitude should be the same as that of Christ Jesus: who made himself nothing, taking the very nature of a servant,

...And...he humbled himself and became obedient to death–even death on a cross!

Philippians 2:5, 7-8

"I want to be a humble person." Words rarely heard and practiced even less. To preach, teach or write about humility is difficult. The listener usually assumes the teacher's expertise in a subject, but this is not written by an expert. Who really has grasped humility? If you think you have it, watch out. However, at the foot of the cross we can see Jesus' example and be moved toward genuine humility. While we may continue to wrestle with pride, Jesus on the cross can break our normal patterns and teach us to walk in humility.

It is often assumed in the world that humility means being quiet, passive, soft, weak, a "push-over," apathetic and without convictions. The "humble" person is the loner in the corner. Does that sound like Jesus to you? It certainly isn't the Jesus I meet in the Gospels. Jesus was a man of passion, purpose and deep convictions. He embraced his task, confronted his opponents, and pressed on resolutely toward his goal. He was no wimp, but he was humble. He was humble on the road to the cross, and he was humble the day he went to the cross.

Jesus first emptied himself and took the very nature of a servant. Though he was in his very nature God, he became a servant to his

Father and to his fellow man. He washed his disciples' feet, touched the leper and obeyed the Father in everything. He did not consider himself too good for such things. He did not think someone else ought to do it.

But then Jesus crowned a life of serving as he *"humbled himself and became obedient to death—even death on a cross!" "Even death on a cross"*—that's the phrase that needs to get our attention. The Old Testament taught that anyone hung on a tree is under a curse by God (Deuteronomy 21:22-23). It was a symbol of God's judgment and rejection. Even though he was innocent and completely obedient, he allowed himself to be cursed. Jesus allowed himself to be rejected by the Father so we wouldn't have to be (2 Corinthians 5:21, Galatians 3:13). He did what he didn't have to and took what he didn't deserve—not because he didn't know what else to do, but because he had his focus on us. He was humble. He didn't argue but obeyed and went. He put his trust in him who judges justly (1 Peter 2:23).

Are you ready to test yourself for humility? (1) How do feel about serving? Do you view yourself as a servant of God, of the Kingdom, of your neighbor? How about of your wife, of your husband, of your enemy? Do you ever feel "too good" for something? Those who are humble are servants and not just outwardly but from the heart. (2) Do you trust God even when doing so means being put in some low position or having to suffer for others? In other words, are you obedient even when it doesn't make you "look good" because you are confident in him who judges justly? There is no real humility without faith. Humility will lead us to places where we can only be sustained by faith.

When you stand at the foot of the cross and see the heart of Jesus, does it change your perspective? Does it still seem so difficult to seek advice? Does it still seem so hard to say, "I'm sorry, forgive me, I have sinned"? When you see him, in humility, taking our curse, can you deliberately sin, stay defensive, hold a grudge or be bitter?

With humility you give up yourself, but in the process you find God and yourself. Look at the biblical answer to four important questions: (1) Where does God dwell? With the humble and contrite (Isaiah 57:15). (2) Who does God esteem? He who is humble and contrite in spirit and trembles at his word (Isaiah 66:2-3). Do you tremble at his Word? Do quiet times change you? Or do you only repent after a "hard talk"? (3) Who receives God's grace? Not the proud, for he opposes them, but instead, those who are humble (James 4:6). Have you ever felt opposed by God? Is it hard for you to feel grace? Many times the opposition we feel is God trying to teach us humility and trust in him. Do people feel you are approachable? Is confession normal for you? Do you really want to experience God's grace? Open your life to a brother or sister. Be real so the grace can come in. (4) Who does God lift up? Those who humble themselves under God's mighty hand (1 Peter 5:5-6). When we resist God, we push away the hand that can help us. During my difficult times, God is the one who lifts me up. God loves me, but he loves me enough to let me learn to be humble. He humbles me, but only so he can lift me up. *"Therefore God exalted him to the highest place"* (Philippians 2:9). Where does humility get you? It took Jesus to the very top, and God will elevate all who are humble to those same heights where they will reign together with Christ.

Do you want God to dwell with you? Do you want God's esteem? Do you want God's grace? Do you want God to lift you up? Get on your knees, get your eyes on the cross, and humble yourself!

FOR FURTHER STUDY

Deuteronomy 8

James 3:13-18, 4:4-10

Titus 3:1-2

Every Day

CAROL MCGUIRK
Paris, France

> Your attitude should be the same as that of Christ Jesus: who made himself nothing, taking the very nature of a servant,
>
> ...And...he humbled himself and became obedient to death–even death on a cross!
>
> Philippians 2:5, 7-8

The cross. Daily. The cross. Every day. The cross not just on Sundays. The cross as a lifestyle. That was Jesus' point.

Do you remember when you decided to die with Jesus in baptism? Do you remember how your heart pounded within you? You were so convinced, so full of faith, so certain of God's all-consuming unconditional love. All disciples have experienced the very same death and the very same resurrection to new life. Before baptism, we became conscious of our spiritual deadness. We were dead in our sins. Then something incredible happened. The cross. It came into view.

Recently when studying the Bible with a friend, I sought to help her understand why Jesus had to die on the cross for us. More than anything, I wanted to show her how much Jesus loves her and how he did what he did so that she could be in a relationship with him. Together we wiped tears from our eyes as she understood for the first time that Jesus died for her personally. What kind of God would work out such a plan? My God and yours.

My friend's response was, "What can I do to deserve this love?"

I told her simply, "Nothing."

There is no act of sacrifice, obedience or devotion to God that can earn you his love. *"For it is by grace that you have been saved, through faith—and this is not from yourselves, it is the gift of God"* (Ephesians 2:8). We should be motivated by an incredible sense of appreciation and thankfulness.

A Savior hanging on a tree because of our sins: unfaithfulness to our spouses, lustful thoughts, abortions, prejudices, bitterness, bad attitudes, jealousy, pride, hatred, cowardice, lack of love, and unbelief. But in baptism we came to the cross, and we were forgiven and raised to a new life (Romans 6:1-4). And we came up and out, grateful for our salvation and determined to live that resurrected life. It was never God's plan for those convictions to quickly dissipate, but rather, they are to become a way of life day after day after day.

The cross and the resurrection were not meant to happen just once. If the cross is not our lifestyle, then sin will be (Romans 6:16). But when the cross is daily, resurrection will be daily.

Daily we are to die to selfishness and be raised to self sacrifice, die to greed and be raised to generosity, die to cowardice and be raised to courage, die to foolishness and be raised to wisdom, die to irresponsibility and be raised to discipline, die to insecurity and be raised to confidence.

Making the cross your lifestyle means dealing quickly with sin. It means admitting sin to yourself and confessing it to God and others. It means repenting quickly and not letting sin drag on for days or even weeks. God wants each of us to have a joy-filled, abundant life that is full of impact. Does that describe your life? If not, maybe it's time to get help and find the solu- tions necessary so that you can change.

When you have a hard time picking up your cross or denying yourself or believing that God is with you, what do you do? Do you run from your feelings? Do you become withdrawn and uncommunicative? Do you overeat, sleep, become rebellious? Or do you seek to be reminded of the love for you that God expressed through the cross? Do you dig into the Word of God? Do you pray until you get back a healthy spiritual perspective? Do you call another close disciple who can help you remember and regain a right attitude? We must simply do whatever it takes to make the cross our lifestyle.

When you see sin in your life, do you have an attitude that says, "I'm willing to do whatever it takes to get the conviction, the desire, the courage and the strength to do as my Lord and Savior has done for me? Is there any sin that you are hanging on to instead of hanging on the cross with Jesus? If so, confess it, and nail it to the cross today! Let the death of Jesus daily motivate and inspire you to die to sin for others.

If we are truly thankful, we will take action and start living everyday from the foot of the cross. We will want to live with him, like him and for him. When we decide to live the cross fully, there is nothing but victory to be found!

FOR FURTHER STUDY

1 Corinthians 15:31
Romans 6:15-23, 8:5-17
Hebrews 3:12-13
Acts 2:42-47
Philippians 1:27
Psalm 145:2

SACRIFICE

Spectators or Sacrifices?

Mary Franz
Minneapolis, Minnesota

> Therefore, I urge you, brothers, in view of God's mercy, to offer your bodies as living sacrifices, holy and pleasing to God —this is your spiritual act of worship.
>
> —Romans 12:1

Sacrifice. The very word frightens many of us. Almost immediately we think of pain, suffering, loss. Because the general attitude toward sacrifice is negative, politicians and other leaders are very hesitant to use it. At the very heart of any kind of sacrifice is the uncomfortable concept of denying yourself something that you like or desire. The world seldom encourages us to sacrifice. Few see it as a virtue to be sought. More often we hear: "Do what feels good." "Make yourself comfortable at all costs." "Get whatever is within your power to possess."

When God calls us to offer ourselves as living sacrifices, what does he mean, and why is it the right thing and the best thing? As human beings, we are naturally the servants of sin (Romans 6:16-17)—we are inclined toward taking for ourselves, not toward giving to others. Sacrifice is a voluntary presentation of ourselves to God to be used for his purposes—to serve him.

Do you want to know what that looks like? Fix your eyes on Jesus. The one who was, in essence, God, gave up his heavenly existence to come to earth—the very earth which was created through him (John 1:3). He sacrificed his comfortable position with God to serve, heal, love, preach the good news and to die on a cross so that we could be with him. He was betrayed, physically beaten, spat upon, crucified and separated from his Father when he took on our sin. It is that separation that ultimately defines true sacrifice for disciples. Unfathomable. Why would he be willing? How could he be willing? The answer resonates through the centuries: undeserved, unconditional love. Two-thousand years later we still don't understand it, but we unmistakably see and hear it.

We can respond in several ways to the sacrifice of Jesus. We can simply bury our heads in the sand and pretend that it never happened. In a word, we can decide to hide from the challenge of the cross and from the life of sacrifice it calls for in us. We can immerse ourselves in other thoughts and crowd the cross out of our lives. If that seems too dishonest, we can face the cross but decide to spectate, standing back with folded arms. The result? Intellectual understanding of the facts, but no personal acceptance of need or of responsibility. This is followed by rationalization and self-justification which meets the all-important need to feel good about ourselves. Interestingly enough, a natural consequence of this disengaging approach is a critical attitude toward others who have made the third decision—the decision to commit. The sacrifice of Jesus was so selfless, so convicting, that soft hearts respond with the desire to sacrifice all. *"For Christ's love compels us, because we are convinced that one died for all, and therefore all died. And he died for all, that those who live should no longer live for themselves but for him who died for them and was raised again"* (2 Corinthians 5:14-15). Hiding is dishonest. Spectating is hypocritical. Committing is powerful.

As we struggle with sacrifice, we need to go to the garden with Jesus and pray with him, *"My Father, if it is possible, may this cup be taken from me. Yet not as I will, but as you will"* (Matthew 26:39). He prayed and prayed until he was ready. Then he said, *"Rise, let us go!"* (Matthew 26:46). He made his decision and committed himself to the cross. The disciples who had walked with Jesus first hid, then spectated, but finally they committed (there is hope for us all!). Once they were convinced of his resurrection, no one, nothing, not even death, would keep them from offering themselves as living sacrifices. They had seen the power of a sacrificial life, and they joined Jesus at the cross.

So what happens when you offer your body as a living sacrifice to God? "I tell you the truth, unless a kernel of wheat falls to the ground and dies, it remains only a single seed. But if it dies, it produces many seeds. The man who loves his life will lose it, while the man who hates his life in this world will keep it for eternal life" (John 12:24-25). What happens is that life truly becomes life. Our joy is multiplied; it affects others, and it ushers us into the presence of God for eternity.

Biblical sacrifice is taking something very valuable to you and totally giving it up because you believe that more good will come from giving it than from grasping it. There was a time several years ago when my husband, Tom, and I sold our possessions to make a move for the sake of the Kingdom. Though it was difficult to part with some things, we did it. Afterwards we were both freed-up and fired-up. We drove to our new home with what we could fit into our small car. We understood God in a deeper way and had peace, trust and joy in our hearts as we drove. God has been faithful to us in our sacrifice. We have received more than we ever gave up. God has not only met our needs, he has always met them abundantly. When you sacrifice your time, money or comfort for him, he will bless your life in ways you could never imagine.

So, we are faced with a decision in light of the cross. What type of sacrifice is he asking of you right now? Is there anything or anyone or any place or any position you are holding on to? Don't hide. Don't be a spectator. Be moved and inspired by the love of Christ, and offer yourself as a living sacrifice. Discover that giving is more glorious than grasping.

FOR FURTHER STUDY

Genesis 22:1-19
Malachi 1:6-14
Matthew 20:26-28
Mark 10:17-31
Acts 20:24
Philippians 3:7-11

SUFFERING

Problem or Possibility?

Kelly Amaya
Boston, Massachusetts

> When they hurled their insults at him, he did not retaliate; when he suffered, he made no threats. Instead, he entrusted himself to him who judges justly.
>
> —1 Peter 2:23

> And the God of all grace, who called you to his eternal glory in Christ, after you have suffered a little while, will himself restore you and make you strong, firm and steadfast.
>
> —1 Peter 5:10

Suffering is a problem for us. We don't like it. We have trouble figuring it out. We try hard to avoid it. But Jesus suffered. The author and perfecter of our faith suffered abandonment, insults, false accusations, flogging, being spat upon, a crown of thorns, rejection and a disgraceful death on the cross. But through it all, God was working. In his suffering Jesus was being perfected for the work of salvation that God sent him to accomplish. Suffering tempts us. We don't handle it well, but Jesus suffered without sinning. How? By keeping his eyes and heart on the goal of heaven and by focusing more on the help being brought to others than the pain he was feeling.

Jesus, through suffering, was made perfect because of his obedience and submission to God. In Gethsemane we see him struggle with his own will, but we also see him triumphantly submit his will to God's (Matthew 26:36-46). Jesus was perfectly obedient, but in his struggle, he shared in our humanity; he became flesh and blood. *"Because he himself suffered when he was tempted, he is able to help those who are being tempted"* (Hebrews 2:18). Our Lord sympathizes with our weaknesses because he *"has been tempted in every way, just as we are—yet was without sin"* (Hebrews 4:15). Jesus was murdered by sinful men without cause, but his heart and mind were full of love, free of resentment and void of hate. One of the most incredible scriptures in the Bible is found in Luke 23:34 because it demonstrates a pure and completely godly response to suffering at the hands of evil men. "Jesus said, *'Father, forgive them, for they do not know what they are doing.'"*

He was able to endure the burden of our sins and a shameful death on the cross because he was sure of what lay ahead for him—heaven. He was able to do it because he knew *"the joy set before him"* (Hebrews 12:2)—the joy of resurrection and reunion with God. He also knew that, through his suffering, he would open the way for us to go to heaven with him. He said, *"I am going there to prepare a place for you"* (John 14:2).

"Why is God doing this to me?" "Is this situation from God or from Satan?" "If God is such a loving God, why does he allow me to suffer so much?"

We spend too much time and energy asking ourselves questions like these—the wrong questions. God's will for Jesus' life was hard. *"It was the Lord's will to crush him and cause him to suffer"* (Isaiah 53:10), yet Jesus was never angry, resentful or rebellious toward God. He accepted God's will for his life and in the same way we need to accept the things that happen in our lives. We should not be so concerned with why we suffer or who causes us to suffer, but we should rather be concerned with responding righteously to the suffering. Jesus simply trusted God. He didn't feel the need to try to make things work out the way that seemed best to him.

"Consider it pure joy, my brothers, when you face trials of many kinds" (James 1:2). In its many forms, suffering is painful when we are experiencing it. However, we must learn not to run from it, but to receive it joyfully, knowing that it is an opportunity for growth and maturity (James 1:3-4). It's also an opportunity to prove the genuineness of our faith (1 Peter 1:6). As I look back on the hard times in my life, I would not want to go through them again, but I am thankful to

God for the good things that I learned through bad experiences. Living with an alcoholic stepfather and experiencing the fear, violence and heartbreak of that situation taught me to have compassion for others who are going through similar things. Experiencing the loss of my mother to cancer was a horrible experience, but it taught me spiritual urgency for those around me. It increased my gratitude for my spiritual family, and it led to my teenaged brother moving in with us and becoming a disciple.

Look for what you can learn through your suffering. Thank God for the good and the bad that comes your way. Allow suffering to train you to be more Christlike, more righteous, as a result of the things you go through. In other words, if you have to suffer, make sure it counts for something—for you and for others.

Have you ever experienced physical pain, abuse, abandonment, emotional pain, deception by a good friend, the loss of a loved one or persecution? Well, so did Jesus. Please don't think that no one understands. Jesus does. Don't feel sorry for yourself. The issue is how did you respond and how will you respond in the future? With every struggle, thank God and strive for righteousness, proving your faith genuine. "*You believe in him and are filled with an inexpressible and glorious joy, for you are receiving the goal of your faith, the salvation of your souls*" (1 Peter 1:8-9). Jesus, for the joy set before him, endured the cross. What will you endure?

FOR FURTHER STUDY

Malachi 1 and 3
Romans 5:1-5
Philippians 3:17-21, 4:10-20
Hebrews 5:7-10
1 Peter 4:12-19

SERVING

If the King Is a Servant

Maria Rogers
Boston, Massachusetts

> Jesus called them together and said, "You know that the rulers of the Gentiles lord it over them, and their high officials exercise authority over them. Not so with you. Instead, whoever wants to become great among you must be your servant, and whoever wants to be first must be your slave—just as the Son of Man did not come to be served, but to serve, and to give his life as a ransom for many."
>
> —Matthew 20:25-28

Kings generally expect to be treated as royalty. They expect to live in the best places and get the best service. They expect to have others clamoring to meet their needs. But the Son of God, King of Kings, and Lord of Lords, becomes flesh and makes his home among us and, remarkably, says he came *"not to be served, but to serve, and give his life as a ransom for many."* What Jesus rightly deserved and what he received while here on the earth were quite different. A close look at Jesus' life brings up one word that distinctly describes him—servant. He had no view of himself other than that of a servant, a slave of God on behalf of man. Jesus didn't resent or resist his role. He humbly and eagerly spent himself for others. When he saw people, he was overwhelmed, not with their needs and desires, but with compassion and the desire to help them. He didn't see them as burdensome. Instead, he saw their burdens of guilt and sin and made himself the ultimate servant by allowing himself to be the sacrifice for sin. He paid the greatest of prices to put our needs ahead of his own.

The culmination of Jesus' life as a servant came when he laid down his life on the cross. Man's ultimate and most desperate need is that of forgiveness and atonement. As a servant, *"he humbled himself and became obedient to death—even death on a cross!"* (Philippians 2:8). It took the greatest of humility and selflessness for him to subject himself to the cruelest of deaths. But Jesus, as a servant, was consumed with pleasing his Master and fulfilling God's desire to reconcile mankind to himself. He prayed in Gethsemane, *"Not my will, but yours be done."* His heart of self-denial was vividly shown as he sweat drops of blood under extreme anguish. He suffered more than is humanly conceivable as he faced his torturous death with both the physical and spiritual implications of the cross. That is why *"God exalted him to the highest place and gave him the name that is above every name, that at the name of Jesus every knee should bow, in heaven and on earth, and under the earth, and every tongue confess that Jesus Christ is Lord"* (Philippians 2:9).

When I think about people who have had a major impact on my life and who have caused my heart to change and to soften, I think of those who have served me. My mother comes to mind immediately as I remember all the times she took care of me as a little girl. For years, from the age of seven to ten, I used to wake up in the middle of the night with throbbing pain in my legs because my bones were growing. It was very painful, and I would cry and moan. She would pick me up, take me into the bathroom, fill up the sink with very warm water, and rub my legs with the water. She sang to me and loved me tenderly, never complaining that she was losing sleep because of me. She served me in countless ways and denied herself to meet my needs. I am moved when I think of all that she has sacrificed for me because of her love.

Nothing moves the human heart more than someone who puts the need of another above his or her own need and willingly serves. It is a rare and precious expression of love. When Jesus washed his disciples' feet, showing them the full extent of his love, they were shocked, humbled and deeply moved. He then, in turn, told them to do the same for others—to be servants. He was teaching them how to have impact.

Jesus has called you and me to be like him and to take on his attitude toward serving others. It is easier to serve someone whom you deeply love and who has served you. But what about your enemy? When Jesus washed their feet, he had the same heart for Judas that he had for the other disciples, fully knowing that Judas would betray him. His serving was not limited to any group or class. He was a servant in heart. Therefore, it was impossible for him not to serve. His very nature was to serve and to deny himself for others.

As disciples of Jesus Christ, we must view ourselves as servants to all—our family members, brothers and sisters, and the lost. Jesus even said that his people will be those who do simple acts of service for *"the least"* among us (Matthew 25:40). Perhaps we enjoy serving a leader or someone important, but do we wholeheartedly serve "the least" as well? At the cross Jesus was the servant of all.

I also find it easier to serve someone when I plan to do so, or when it is convenient. But my heart is revealed when I am unexpectedly asked to serve, interrupting my schedule. Do I then consider it a privilege and honor to fulfill my role as a servant? When those surprises come, is it clear that I am, in my nature, a servant?

If the King is a servant, what does that mean for the rest of us? Let us capture the heart of Jesus and become servants in the truest sense, longing to be *"living sacrifices, holy and pleasing to God"* (Romans 12:1).

FOR FURTHER STUDY

Matthew 20:20-28, 25:31-46
John 21:1-14
Romans 15:1-4

SERVING

The Surprise of Serving

Doug Webber
Los Angeles, California

> Your attitude should be the same as that of Christ Jesus: Who, being in very nature God, did not consider equality with God something to be grasped, but made himself nothing, taking the very nature of a servant, being made in human likeness. And being found in appearance as a man, he humbled himself and became obedient to death—even death on a cross!
> —Philippians 2:5-8

Jesus had such an amazing attitude toward saving the world from its sin that though he was deity, he became humanity; though he was the greatest, he became the least; though he was a king, he became a servant. Jesus took the form of a servant not to conceal but to reveal who God is.

If Jesus had not first become a servant, he would not have been able powerfully to become our Savior through the cross. There were two types of servants in the biblical world. One was the type of servant known as the "hired servant," who had certain rights (see Genesis 29:15-30). The other was the "bond servant" who had no rights, received no wages, had no appeal and was the outright property of the master (see Luke 17:7-10). There were several circumstances under which a Jew might be reduced to a bond servant. These included: theft, being unable to make proper restitution, poverty and losing mortgaged property with the need to sell himself to someone else. In such a state, these people became the "nothings" of Jewish society who were the ones most looked down on. This was the type of servant Jesus *willfully* and *purposefully* became according to

Philippians 2, opening the way for his work for us at Golgotha. Jesus was able to scorn the shame of the cross because he had first made himself nothing, taking the form of a servant for us.

His willingness to become a servant and his willingness to go to the cross issued from the same heart. As a servant, he was driven by a desire to obey God and a desire to provide for man's greatest need. Yes, at the cross there would be pain, agony and abandonment; but at the cross he would fulfill his deepest desire and greatest sense of obligation. At the cross there would be triumph because in his heart he was a servant and wanted nothing more than to serve.

I recently challenged myself to find out how I could become a stronger disciple of Jesus. Searching the Scriptures, I found many areas in which I needed, in deeper and more consistent ways, to make myself nothing. I found I was a lot more familiar with making myself something than with making myself nothing.

I began to realize that if I were to become nothing in a number of areas, the transformation in my character would have to be preceded by suffering. It would be painful to sleep less, take on more responsibility, look less toward my own needs and interests, and be more humble toward others. The challenge, I realized, was not simply to endure this process, but to endure it with a great attitude. Isaiah 53:11 says, referring to Jesus' dying on the cross, *"After the suffering of his soul, he will see the light of life and be satisfied; by his knowledge my righteous servant will justify many, and he will bear their iniquities."* Jesus understood that through becoming a servant and fulfilling a servant's work, he would ultimately be satisfied. That surely helped motivate him to serve and must also help motivate you and me, as well.

Jesus makes it clear that the degree of true greatness in his kingdom is determined by the degree to which one has become a bondservant (Mark 10:35-44). Do we hear that? This greatness comes not through self-exaltation but through self-denial, with God thereby exalting one to true greatness. Do we deeply believe this? Are you a servant in your workplace? Are you a servant at home? Are you known as a servant among other disciples? Will others quickly turn to you because they know you have a heart to serve?

We find Jesus himself leading us in this area: *"And being found in appearance as a man, he humbled himself and became obedient to death—even death on a cross! Therefore God exalted him to the highest place and gave him the name that is above every name"* (Philippians 2:8-9). The Bible says he was given not just any place, but the highest place! God wants us to aspire to greatness in his Kingdom, but he wants us to know that the road to greatness must pass through the valley of servanthood. Let's forget about climbing up the ladder of success and focus instead on climbing down the ladder until we get to the position of servant.

FOR FURTHER STUDY

Isaiah 52:13-53
Matthew 10:24-25
Galatians 5:13-15
James 1:9-11
1 Peter 4:7-11, 5:2-4

DETERMINATION

Seeing It Through

Jimmy Rogers
Boston, Massachusetts

> As the time approached for him to be taken up to heaven, Jesus resolutely set out for Jerusalem.
>
> —Luke: 9:51

It is not that hard to start something, but it takes character to finish. As we look at Jesus, we find that kind of rich character. He kept going in the face of great pain and opposition. He refused to stop until his task was finished. Jesus had a mission—to save men and women from their sins—and he was determined to see it through. Praise God!

But what did it take for him to reach his goal? Nothing less than death—on a cross—on a garbage dump outside Jerusalem. He had to be determined.

Since he was the Son of God, our first thought may be that he walked through life as if it were a breeze. A closer look shows us the greatest of all heroes. His character and strength were focused on what he had to endure and overcome while living his life and going to his ultimate test, the cross.

Jesus was fully God, and yet fully man. *"For in Christ all the fullness of the Deity lives in bodily form"* (Colossians 2:9). We only get a glimpse of the life of Jesus through the gospels. *"Jesus did many other things as well. If every one of them were written down, I suppose that even the whole world would not have room for the books that would be written"* (John 21:25). But what we have is sufficient to show us that Jesus was just like you and me. Everyday he battled with temptations—sometimes called "the pressures of life" but biblically described as *"the devil's schemes."* The struggle was real, but to give in was inconceivable. In Hebrews 4:15, the Bible says, *"For we do not have a high priest who is unable to sympathize with our weaknesses, but we have one who has been tempted in every way, just as we are—yet was without sin."* He faced it all. With dull disciples he could have become impatient. Exhausted after a long journey, he could have become selfish. And yet, he never gave in.

How could he stay focused and so determined to overcome? Hebrews 5:7 gives us a clue: *"During the days of Jesus' life on earth, he offered up prayers and petitions with loud cries and tears to the one who could save him from death, and he was heard because of his reverent submission."* Deep in his relationship with God, Jesus shed tears for the lost, tears for the people he met and healed, tears for his disciples who needed to remain faithful, tears for his family who thought that he was crazy, and tears for the children and what their future would hold without him. With loud cries he asked God to help him be faithful to all of these. Knowing that God heard his cries and saw his tears, he found victory over discouragement, anxiety, doubt and loneliness. At times he had no one but God. But God was enough—enough to keep him from sin and enough to strengthen him for the cross.

When I first studied the Bible and considered becoming a disciple, I understood how important it was to count the cost. I heard Jesus in Luke 14:28-30 and knew he was making sure that I had the faith, heart and conviction to finish what I had started and keep him Lord of my life no matter what happened. Jesus knew that if we aren't determined and resolute about following him, we just won't last. Like a marriage, life with Jesus must begin with an irrevocable decision and a lifetime commitment. We must put our hands to the plow and never look back. We must see his dreams for our lives and then pursue them with fire in our eyes.

But that initial decision must be renewed and refreshed. Like Jesus, we need times when our doubts, fears, anxieties and loneliness are addressed and dealt with decisively. Like Jesus, we must have heartfelt and emotional times with God when he sees our tears and hears our loud cries. In the parable of the sower, Jesus spoke of those who initially accept the Word but get distracted by life's worries, mishaps and pleasures. Distraction, which looks deceptively innocent, is disastrous because it is the exact opposite of determination. Distracted people don't seem bent on evil, but what can they accomplish? Only communion with heaven will give us the perspective to stay focused and determined on earth.

Sometimes, aware of our ineffectiveness, we focus on what we should be doing but neglect our relationship with God. The result here is also devastating because we begin to depend on our own power, and that causes us to feel empty and overwhelmed—not exactly a formula for joyful perseverance.

There are surely some things in your life you have been determined to accomplish. You wanted something so badly that you were not going to let anything stop you. Unfortunately, not all those things you pursued were righteous, but looking back you can see a picture of determination. Now go after the will of God with that same set of the jaw and that same look in your eye. Recognize that there will be foes within and foes without, but make up your mind, like Jesus did, that you are going to reach your goal.

As it was with Jesus, so it will be with you and me. We will have to fight some tough battles, but let us settle in our hearts one issue: We will never quit. We will reach our goal.

FOR FURTHER STUDY

Luke 13:32

1 Corinthians 15:58

2 Corinthians 4:7-12, 16-18

Philippians 3:12-14

2 Timothy 4:7-8

PERSECUTION

Mistreatment but Not Misery

Laurie Tranchell
Hyannis, Massachusetts

> Let us fix our eyes on Jesus, the author and perfecter of our faith, who for the joy set before him endured the cross, scorning its shame, and sat down at the right hand of the throne of God. Consider him who endured such opposition from sinful men, so that you will not grow weary and lose heart.
>
> —Hebrews 12:2-3

Beaten, flogged, spat upon, slapped, mocked, insulted, laughed at, rejected, lied about, struck with fists, ridiculed. Persecution—on the cross Jesus faced it all. Physical and emotional torment—he endured it all, scorning its shame. Most amazing of all, he faced it for the joy set before him and stayed focused on that joy. Included among the lessons we learn at the foot of the cross are some powerful ones to help us with our attitudes toward persecution.

First, we see clearly that there is no way to be righteous enough, wise enough or loving enough to avoid persecution. The cross was the climax of our Savior's persecution on earth. Throughout his life he faced it daily from governing authorities, religious authorities and even members of his own family. *"The world cannot hate you,"* Jesus said once to his physical brothers, *"but it hates me because I testify that what it does is evil"* (John 7:7). The cross reminds us of the world's reaction to truth. We cannot follow Jesus and not get that same reaction. *"In fact, everyone who wants to live a godly life in Christ Jesus will be persecuted"* (2 Timothy 3:12).

But in Jesus we see more than the inevitability of persecution, we see how to respond to it. We never see in him a hint of retaliation, bitterness or self-pity.

1 Peter 2:21 calls us to follow Jesus and his example on the cross, and then verses 22-23 describe the attitude he had: *"When they hurled their insults at him, he did not retaliate; when he suffered, he made no threats. Instead, he entrusted himself to him who judges justly."* Persecution just brought out his best.

Absence of malice—yes. But as he endured opposition, Jesus also maintained his completely selfless concern for those around him. As the religious leaders were mocking him, people were insulting him and even the two robbers who were crucified with him *"heaped insults on him"* (Matthew 27:44), he asked God to *"forgive them, for they do not know what they are doing"* (Luke 23:34). Jesus takes time to acknowledge and forgive one of the robbers hanging with him when he tells him, *"Today you will be with me in paradise"* (Luke 23:43). Jesus was concerned for his mother as he looked down upon her and turned her over to the care of the apostle John (John 19:27).

But how did he get through the cruel and vicious attacks with such grace? *"He entrusted himself to him who judges justly"* (1 Peter 2:23), and he kept his focus on the joy that would be his (Hebrews 12:2). These men didn't know what they were doing, but God did. These men were not in control. God was. These men would not win. God would. Such trust is the key to endurance in the midst of attack.

Teaching us about hearts in the parable of the sower in Matthew 13:21, Jesus says that one of the tests we must face is persecution. The person with no roots *"lasts only a short time. When trouble or persecution comes because of the word, he quickly falls away."* Persecution exposes our hearts. The heart with a root that goes down deep into the word of God will actually be strengthened, not weakened, by persecution.

What is our attitude when we are faced with a critical media report, called a name or denied some opportunity because of our faith? How do we respond when our families reject us? Do we shrink back? Do we feel sorry for ourselves? How do we feel toward our persecutors? We must learn to respond as Jesus did, with love and concern for others and a deep trust in his Father's will.

When I was two days old as a Christian, the head of student activities at my school called me into his office and proceeded to warn me about the church of which I had just become a part. Sitting in his office that day, I had a choice as to how I was going to react—whether to panic and get emotional or to trust God and be strengthened. I chose to be strengthened, and God didn't fail me.

Later that same day my advisor told me that by joining the church, I had ruined my career and my reputation with the university. Again the choice was there. I remember feeling as if God had leaned down and given me a hug as a baby Christian. I decided to allow a difficult time to draw me closer to God and not allow a doubting spirit to enter my heart. Later that same year, some of my close friends did a skit in a school show mocking me and my Bible discussion group. Sitting in the audience, I was hurt and shocked and fought to have compassion and love for my friends. I sat there and prayed for them to someday understand the truth.

Since that challenging beginning, things have only gotten more intense, but the lesson that I learned in my first few months as a Christian has been one I will never forget: When mistreatment comes, draw closer to God. Only with his help and strength can we respond like Jesus. If the roots of our hearts go deeply into God's word, persecution will just bring the best out of us.

FOR FURTHER STUDY

Matthew 5:1-12, 13:1-23
Romans 8:28-39
2 Timothy 3:10-17

IN THE
WORKING WORLD

Lasting Impact

Daniel H. Bathon, Jr.
Chadds Ford, Pennsylvania

> Since, then, you have been raised with Christ, set your hearts on things above, where Christ is seated at the right hand of God. Set your minds on things above, not on earthly things. For you died, and your life is now hidden with Christ in God.
>
> —Colossians 3:1-3

From the minute we are born we are inundated by the influence of earthly things. The newspaper, the television, the school, the workplace—all deployed to win us over in a massive indoctrination. We learn very early the worldly things to pursue: fame, fortune and material possessions. We are robotized into rote responses to please our earthly mentors at school, work and play. A "value system" is consciously and subconsciously woven into our character.

But at the cross, Jesus refutes all that we have learned and all that the world says is so valuable. He shows us a totally different way, and he offers us a choice. He puts the emphasis on service, sacrifice and spiritual power. There is perhaps no greater challenge for a disciple than to live out this radical message of Jesus in the workplace—that stronghold of the world's thinking.

Before you decide Jesus just doesn't understand the high-powered and high-pressured world out there, look again. His connections were in the highest places (John 1:1); his ability to move the masses was unparalleled (Matthew 7:28), and his understanding of what it takes to succeed was clear and unwavering (John 12:23-24). Intimidating forces constantly pressured him to compromise or give up, but he stayed with his task until it was totally finished (John 19:30). Even the cross, a sign of failure to everyone around him, became a stunning victory (as he had planned and prayed). When he speaks, we have reason to listen.

Taking the cross into the workplace begins with understanding who we are as we get up each day. We have received the greatest promotion we can ever attain. Because he died for us, we have a position *in Christ*—a position more important than any found in some "dream career." No, our great ability and great performance did not get us here, but we are here, thank God, nonetheless. In what other job could you find eternal security and unlimited benefits?

Because we have the "ultimate connection" we can *"set our hearts on things above."* The work environment usually encourages earthly things such as selfish ambition, greed, malice, lying, lust, sexual immorality, envy, jealousy and the like. It is one thing to stop committing these sins; it is quite another not to have your heart there.

To set your heart is like pouring a foundation in concrete. Have you ever pushed against a foundation after it has been set? It is immovable. In the same way when earthly influences push at your heart, you should be concentrating on heavenly things, always focused, unswerving in your commitment to achieve the goal.

Many of us spend more time at work than any other single place. If we aren't living the cross here, how can we be living it at all? The tests are often great, but the message of the cross is greater.

On Wall Street, the biggest challenge I faced was keeping my convictions always before me. I was trained to do whatever was necessary to reach my goals. The world only limited me by what would look bad if I were caught. Being crucified with Christ meant radical change. For instance, I often "shaded the truth" to make money on sales. I had to identify the sin as lying. To understand that I was a liar was much harder than thinking of myself as a "truth shader," but this was only the beginning. Now I had to hate the lying. My first reaction was, "But how will I make as much money if I only make the honest sale?" This struggle required me to develop the same confidence that Jesus had in God's ability to save him from death. Setting my mind on things above meant having faith that God could make me even more successful if I were faithful to his Son's message. My desire could not be for earthly gain or material rewards. I had to learn to desire the heavenly rewards that come from above.

Another challenge is time commitment. It is so easy to get caught up in our work, and that is definitely what some employers expect. While every disciple needs to work hard, the question is, are we working to glorify God or to exalt ourselves? *"Whatever you do, work at it with all your heart, as working for the Lord, not for men"* (Colossians 3:23). Working to get a promotion, to earn more money or to gain material possessions is to work toward earthly goals. If your heart is set on pleasing the Lord, however, and you also gain these things, thank God. But what is the motivation in your heart? This can easily be tested when you consider if you would be willing to give up these things. Consider the story of the rich young ruler (Matthew 19:16-30). Why do you spend so much time at work? Is it to please your boss, yourself or God?

As disciples, our lives are hidden with Christ, but the pressures of work can push us toward compromise. In an environment of foul language, filthy jokes, constant negative thinking, out-of-town travel and the temptation of sexual immorality, the only way to survive is to be hidden in Christ and intolerant of hidden sin. If our minds are set on the things above, we not only survive but thrive.

When the toughest challenges come and when being a disciple seems to be too radical, just remember that Jesus is the important person. All of our other inside connections are secondary to him. He is the Chairman of the Board. If Jesus had to die, then you will also. How could our temporary work on earth be more important than Jesus and the eternal things of heaven? If we compromise the cross at work, how will we ever overcome the world?

FOR FURTHER STUDY

Daniel 1, 4:19-37
Matthew 23:1-12
Philippians 1:27
Colossians 3:22-25
James 2:1-13, 3:13-18

Not for Adults Only

Julie Bathon
Chadds Ford, Pennsylvania

> Near the cross of Jesus stood his mother....When Jesus saw his mother there, and the disciple whom he loved standing nearby, he said to his mother, "Dear woman, here is your son," and to the disciple, "Here is your mother." From that time on, this disciple took her into his home.
>
> —John 19:25-27

What a heart-wrenching scene this is for Mary as she watches. Put yourself in her shoes at the foot of this cross on which her son Jesus is being crucified. Feel her overwhelming sorrow, her grief, her anguish. Perhaps she was reminded of Simeon's words spoken some 33 years earlier when she presented her newborn to him, *"a sword will pierce your own soul too,"* the old priest had said (Luke 2:35). Imagine your firstborn son, a precious gift from God, being tortured this way. Feel the pain, the devastation, perhaps even the despair she might have been feeling.

However, even from the cross Jesus shows his concern for his mother. That had to help. But why didn't he protect her from the whole experience? Why didn't he use his power to make sure she wouldn't have to see such things and feel such pain? Not only was Jesus willing to go through the heartbreaking experience of the cross, but he was willing to let his mother go through it with him. Why? Because his mother, like the rest of the world, needed to be saved. Because his mother, like all of us, needed to understand the high cost of salvation. Because his mother, as a disciple of Jesus, needed to understand how far we all must be willing to go for the salvation of others.

Jesus and Mary's relationship reminds us that no relationship is an end in itself and no relationship is exempt from the costs of discipleship. Such bonds are special. They bring good feelings to the heart. But we must never forget that they always have a higher purpose. From the mystery of the virgin birth to that brutal scene on Calvary, God was at work in this relationship to accomplish his purpose. Once through the crucifixion, Mary would be a woman with deeper convictions, with a profound understanding of what it means to always carry around in our bodies the death of Jesus (2 Corinthians 4:10).

At the foot of the cross we learn a vital lesson: Families are for God. They exist for his purposes and his plans.

⁂

At the cross, Jesus and his mother teach us that the ultimate goal for our families must not be educational prowess, athletic achievement or worldly happiness, but an eternal relationship with God. The cross calls us to lay down our lives so our husbands, our wives and our children will not only be saved but will learn to lay down their lives so that others might spend eternity with God.

Being a Christian parent doesn't mean you try to spare your children the cross; it means you show them how to get on it. Do you teach your children that God has a plan for their lives? Do they see you sacrifice to bring them to salvation? Do they see you sacrifice your time, your worldly desires, your money, your sleep—all for the lost?

Some time ago I had unavoidably scheduled two Bible studies with non-Christians during a time I usually spend with my kids. Before I left them with a babysitter, I apologized to them for this. Both my son D.H., 9 at the time, and my daughter Grace, 8, said, "Oh, that's okay, Mom. We know you're doing it for God." Having felt so guilty and torn, I then had tears in my eyes. Their response also taught their 4-year-old sister their hearts for God.

As parents, it is often much harder to teach or to call our children to sacrifice than it is to call ourselves to sacrifice. Do you teach your children to sacrifice? Are you willing to let them be sacrificial? Are they learning from Jesus how valuable this quality is and how right it is for all of us?

Are you teaching your kids to sacrifice their worldly desire to retaliate when other kids tease, taunt or even bully them? Kids can be so cruel. Each of our children has already experienced the pain of a "best friend" suddenly turning on them. They have endured the unceasing sarcasm and unkind words about what they wear and what they look like. Dan and I have had to wrestle through our initial worldly reaction to want to protect our kids. Our immediate response to the pain our children feel when things happen to them in the world is to protect them from it. To rush to school and "speak" to the mean kid or even to teach our kids hurtful responses to say back to their tormentors. Do you struggle with wanting your kids to get back at, or get even with, a bully? Or are you teaching them that Jesus taught us, *"love your enemies, do good to those who hate you,...pray for those who mistreat you"* (Luke 6:27-28)?

Are you praying with your children to love the people who are mean to them or hurt them? Are you always looking to Jesus' example? Are you getting advice from other Christian parents on how you can make your children's enemies their friends? Are you teaching your children to care about even the souls of their enemies?

Are you teaching your kids to sacrifice their sleep sometimes for God and be happy, joyful and obedient even when tired? Or are you allowing or even encouraging them to give in to their worldly desire to crave comfort, to be inflexible or to be grouchy when tired?

As parents we are compelled because of the cross to be sacrificial ourselves and to call our children to be sacrificial. To watch our children sacrifice for God can be painful, but it is a lesson they must learn.

We have been entrusted with the very souls of our children. And though a sword may pierce our own souls, let us keep focused on the cross. To the world it is foolishness, but to us who are being saved, it is the power of God.

FOR FURTHER STUDY

Genesis 22:1-19
Deuteronomy 6:1-9
1 Samuel 2:12-36
Matthew 19:13-15
Luke 2:41-52

PART III

Knowing God

Nearer my God to Thee
nearer to Thee?
Even tho' it be
a cross that raises me;
still all my song shall be,
nearer my God to Thee.
—Sarah F. Adams

Nothing but the Best

Adrienne Scanlon
Salem, New Hampshire

> Since you call on a Father who judges each man's work impartially, live your lives as strangers here in reverent fear. For you know that it was not with perishable things such as silver or gold that you were redeemed from the empty way of life handed down to you from your forefathers, but with the precious blood of Christ, a lamb without blemish or defect.
> —1 Peter 1:17-19

"Going along with human nature." "Doing what comes naturally." "Getting in touch with who we really are." "If it feels good, do it." "Be true to yourself."

Ever hear those ideas? Ever get tempted to follow them? But where do all these modern shibboleths lead us? Do they really change our lives? How about a more radical approach? How about seeking the nature of God and seeking to understand what comes naturally to God?

When Jesus' blood was shed on that cross, God was challenging us to reconsider our empty way of life and all of our empty philosophies. He was opening his heart and revealing his nature. He was imploring us to be like him—to imitate anything and everything about him.

What a person is willing to give reveals a lot about the person. What God gave revealed a great deal about God. The apostle Peter was on a mountain top with Jesus when he heard the voice of God the Father expressing the depth of his paternal love: *"This is my son, whom I love; with him I am well pleased"* (2 Peter 1:17). What an experience! We've all seen a father's eyes light up when he holds his son for the first time or shows off his boy, his "best buddy," to his friends and family. Jesus was the perfect Son, the image of his Father, *"the radiance of God's glory and the exact representation of his being"* (Hebrews 1:3). He was the cherished Son, the only Son.

God's willing, planned and gracious sacrifice of this Son provides us with a powerful insight into the nature of God: He is willing to *give his very best*. At the cross he was essentially crying out, "Please understand how much I love you and that you are each worth my best effort." The problem of sin was so great that nothing less would blot it out. But so great was his commitment and so generous was his heart that God was undeterred by the enormous price.

God's precious and costly sacrifice seeks and demands a response. No wonder Peter writes, *"For this very reason, make every effort to add to your faith goodness; and to goodness, knowledge; and to knowledge, self-control; and to self-control, perseverance; and to perseverance, godliness; and to godliness, brotherly kindness; and to brotherly kindness, love"* (2 Peter 1:5-7).

"Make every effort"—the only appropriate response to a God whose nature is to always give his best. But what is your response? Are your personal moments of meditated, prayerful interaction with him sleepy or energized? Are you honestly seeking his kingdom first? Are you striving for personal righteousness? At those personal crossroads of life, is his will utmost in your mind?

Choosing one or two specific areas mentioned in 2 Peter 1:5-7, you can decide to strive for excellence—today. Motivated by God's sacrifice and example, we can increase our faith and our self-control each and every day. The result of this daily, zealous pursuit of excellence will be that our character will begin to reflect the nature of God.

Now that your minds and hearts are prepared for excellence, it is time to determine what will trip you up and cause you to fall short of giving your best. What are the sins that plague you? By labeling certain activities and attitudes "sinful," God has warned us against those things that would weaken our character, steal our energy and undermine our determination. Peter concludes, *"Therefore, prepare your minds for action; be self-controlled; set your hope fully on the grace to be given you when Jesus Christ is revealed. As obedient children, do not conform to the evil desires you had when you lived in ignorance. But just as he who called you is holy, so be holy in all you do"* (1 Peter 1:13-15).

Are you imitating God's attitude toward sin? Do you want to blot out those useless, tiresome, sinful patterns that rob you of your joy and your power as a Christian? As you face God today at the foot of the cross, determine to have a godly, zealous hatred of sin in your life. Choose one or two specific areas in which you want to repent. In response to his best, decide you will give your best.

"God's nature." "Doing what comes unnaturally." "Getting in touch with who we really can be." "If it is excellent, do it." "Be true to God." "A new philosophy." "A blood-bought philosophy."

FOR FURTHER STUDY

Mark 14:1-9

Romans 5:12-21, 6:23, 14:19

Ephesians 4:1-6

Philippians 4:8-9

FAITH

Trusting in Trial

Joanne Webber
Los Angeles, California

"He committed no sin, and no deceit was found in his mouth." When they hurled their insults at him, he did not retaliate; when he suffered, he made no threats. Instead, he entrusted himself to him who judges justly .
—1 Peter 2:22-23

Living by faith is not easy. We have questions, and we like to have answers: "What will happen?" "What will I get?" "Will I be happy?" We carefully plan and do all we can to feel in control. We get security from our research and our knowledge.

To follow Jesus Christ we must live by faith (Romans 1:17). But that sounds risky and by nature, most of us are not risk takers. Faith is the assurance and certainty of things that we do not see, but we like to live by what we can see.

The cross was a test of faith for Jesus. When he cried out in the Garden of Gethsemane and experienced the silence of God, it was a test of faith. When he was beaten and hung on the cross, it was a test of faith. Jesus believed in the plan of God. He believed in the resurrection to come, but he could not see it. He could only see the blood, the pain, the faces of mockers and the dismay of his "loyal" followers. His faith was tested by distress, agony and aloneness. When he quoted from Psalm 22, *"My God, my God, why have you forsaken me?" he had to feel what David said later in that passage: "I am a worm and not a man, scorned by men and despised by the people."* When we see Jesus on the cross, we see faith under seige. But we also see faith that endured. We see faith that stayed strong and was not disappointed (Psalm 22:5).

The cross was hard to face, but the faith that took Jesus to the cross was blessed by God. At the cross Jesus paid the price for our sin. In the resurrection God substantiated everything Jesus had claimed and everything the prophets had predicted. The cross and the resurrection give us reasons for faith in all God's promises. At the cross Jesus shows us that faith in the most difficult moments will be rewarded.

As I reflect on life, I see three situations that we find ourselves in: positive, challenging and tragic. It is a funny thing how my faith seems to grow quickly in positive cirucumstances. It is easy at those times to attribute the good things to God. At such times, I don't have much trouble believing that *"in all things God works for the good of those who love him"* (Romans 8:28).

However, when circumstances are more difficult, the questions surface. I find myself asking God, "Why is this happening?" But these are the very times when faith can mature the most and have the greatest impact. These are the times to fix our eyes on the faith that took Jesus to the cross and through it.

As we go through a challenging situation, financial hardship, the loss of a job, the loss of a relationship, or an illness, the faithful response is to ask, "What good can God work from this?"

Perhaps our faith gets most severely tested during the tragic situations in our lives. When I lost a baby, I knew that it was my most difficult test of faith. It was the most intense emotional time of my life. During this time, I remember having to guard my heart closely and having to focus carefully on what God was trying to teach me personally. Especially during this time, I wanted my faith to be an inspiration to others. I constantly reminded myself that getting angry at God would be so easy, but it would also be so wrong. Faith accepts the situation, asks God for help, and believes that God's power will be sufficient for us. When others see the strength of our faith, they are inspired to increase their faith in God. As Jesus went through the most difficult time in his life, hanging on the cross, he inspired faith in others, including the thief who died with him and a centurion who was putting him to death. The way he died gave others the opportunity for life.

As we reflect on the cross, we see the unwavering faith of Jesus. As we further reflect on the resurrection, we see the reward and the fulfillment of that faith. What situations are you going through right now that require you to imitate the faith of Jesus? Are you facing some impossible odds? Do you see your difficulties as burdens God shouldn't allow, or as tremendous opportunities to demonstrate faith?

FOR FURTHER STUDY

2 Timothy 1:8-12, 4:6-8
Hebrews 4:14-16, 11-12
1 Peter 1:3-9

LOVING THE LOST

Don't Come Down!

Brian Scanlon
Salem, New Hampshire

> Those who passed by hurled insults at him, shaking their heads and saying, "You who are going to destroy the temple and build it in three days, save yourself! Come down from the cross, if you are the Son of God!"
>
> In the same way the chief priests, the teachers of the law and the elders mocked him. "He saved others," they said, "but he can't save himself! He's the King of Israel! Let him come down now from the cross, and we will believe in him."
>
> —Matthew 27:39-42

Jesus had committed his entire life *"to seek and to save what was lost"* (Luke 19:10). He had fought through every temptation for thirty-plus years to be found without sin and give meaning to these otherwise senseless final hours: The only man who had never sinned was dying for all men who had horribly sinned. The eternal redemption of mankind was at hand. It was merely a question of hours. Yet, as the cries rose up from the ruthless crowd surrounding the cross, certain words must have stood out: *"Save yourself....Come down from the cross...."* Humiliating words. Penetrating words. Tempting words. And Jesus heard every one. If there had been a man in the crowd who understood the eternal significance of the moment, he would have cried back, "No, Jesus! Don't come down! *Don't come down!"*

Jesus did not come down, but what if he had? Surely we are mistaken if we think that Jesus wasn't tempted to do so. In fact, it may very well have been Satan's final and most furious attack, that long-awaited most opportune time (Luke 4:13). Jesus could have saved himself. Both he and Satan knew it. He still could have called down those twelve legions of angels (Matthew 26:53) to gloriously lift him from the cross and put everyone in their place. Perhaps he was tempted to save himself and let everyone else fend for themselves. After all, was it really worth giving up his life for so many who seemed so unwilling to respond? Or maybe the real temptation was to come down from the cross in the hope that they would believe, as they said. Simply put, for whatever reason, if Jesus had come down, it would have been over—no hope of salvation in sight. Heaven cried out, "Don't come down! *Don't come down!*" And he didn't.

The question had actually been settled the night before in a garden (Matthew 26:36-46). Though he knew all along what awaited him and had begun to speak openly about it, this moment was inevitable. Alone in a garden. What he said to his disciples was true for himself, *"The spirit is willing, but the body is weak."* In his flesh, Jesus did not want to die—not like that. The struggle lasted hours into the night. Alone in a garden. Loud cries and tears (Hebrews 5:7). Sweat turned into blood (Luke 22:44). He knew it had to come to this. He could not save himself and save others. The cross was the only way. *"Father,... not as I will, but as you will."* Surely other temptations would come before it was over, but he was ready. He had decided. He would not come down until it was finished. And he didn't.

But what kept him up there? What made him decide to go there in the first place? Of course Jesus loved his Father. Nothing could stop him from doing his Father's will in order to please him. But why was this the Father's will? If it is true that God so loved the world that he gave his one and only Son (John 3:16), then it can be said that Jesus so loved the world that he gave his one and only life. That's it. That's why. Love. He cared so deeply for others. Compassionate love. He saw our need and responded. Unconditional love. He responded, in spite of the pain, not knowing how we would respond. As Jesus hung on the cross, he knew he was bringing the hope of salvation to the multitudes he had taught, to the sick he had healed and to the children who had come to him. To you and me. Improving our lives wasn't enough. We needed to be saved. We needed to be loved. Saving love. Thanks, Jesus, for not coming down.

And now we need to figure out where we are. Right now. It was never to be any different for us than it had been for Jesus. He calls us to continue to seek the lost he died to save, saying, *"If anyone would come after me, he must deny himself and take up his cross daily and follow me. For whoever wants to save his life will lose it"* (Luke 9:23). The mission is the same. The cross is ours. The temptations will come, but we must never come down. We cannot save ourselves and save others. There is no other way.

If you're not convinced of that, spend a night in a garden. And struggle—to love. We must quit looking for some new, easy approach and decide to love. We'd better decide daily because daily the world is telling us differently. Aren't you frequently tempted to say nothing to the person beside you who knows little or nothing of the love of God? Are you tempted to compromise in the hope of influencing friends or family members who criticize your commitment? When studying the Bible with some "difficult" person, are you tempted to strike out and put him in his place? Have you ever felt as if no one was open and you were wasting your time trying? Have you ever thought of waiting until you were sure the person would become a Christian before investing yourself?

The world is screaming out, "Save yourself! Come down from your cross!" Jesus is crying back, *"Don't come down!"*

What are you going to do? It will determine the eternal destiny of many others. You love people too much to come down. Make the decision Jesus did. Make it again tomorrow and the next day. And one day soon someone will thank you for not coming down.

FOR FURTHER STUDY

Luke 19:1-10

Romans 9:1-4, 10:1-3

1 Corinthians 9:12-22

Hebrews 12:4-14, 13:11-14

OVERCOMING

Turning the Tables

John McGuirk
Paris, France

> Since the children have flesh and blood, he [Jesus] too shared in their humanity so that by his death he might destroy him who holds the power of death—that is, the devil.
>
> —Hebrews 2:14

Satan had his hold on us! We had been tempted by the tempter because of our own evil desires. We were dragged away from what was right and good. We were enticed to enjoy shortsighted and short-lived pleasures. We sinned and kept on sinning. Sometimes willingly, even wholeheartedly and other times doing the things that we least wanted to do. Losing the battle more times than winning, we found ourselves powerless, prisoners of the prince of this world.

Satan's massive claws had been choking the life and breath out of us for years. After deceiving and abusing us, he manipulated and used us to do his dirty work. And right about the time when he looked to finish us off, the man named Jesus came out of nowhere and ripped him from our backs. He who had the power to put us to death was defeated, destroyed with one fatal blow...at the cross.

Jesus' presence in this world was an all-out assault on death and the devil. He came to turn the tables on Satan once and for all. Even to the casual observer it became abundantly clear that Jesus had come to deal with the greatest of all questions and fears—death. Jesus revealed his power and authority over death. He healed many on the edge of death. He spoke at great length about death (John 5:21-30). He claimed to be the only solution for death (John 6:53-57). He raised the dead (John 11). He believed his death would bring others life (John 12:23-25). But when he died, to almost everyone it looked as though evil had won.

Double- and triple-teamed even from birth by Satan, who regarded him as public enemy number one, Jesus never gave in to sin, not even once. Satan pulled out all the stops, and he stopped at nothing. He had the home court advantage, and Jesus was in his deadly sights at all times. The prowling lion was waiting for just one bad day, even one bad moment, but it never came. Tempted and tested in *"every way, just as we are"* (Hebrews 4:15), Jesus suffered, struggled, cried out and submitted during the days of his life and up to his last breath (Hebrews 5:7). He never earned the wages of sin and did not deserve to die, and, in fact, didn't have to die. However, as Satan lost in his effort to pull Jesus into sin, he no doubt took satisfaction in seeing Jesus accused, despised, abused and executed. Watching so many people doing his bidding had to give him a feeling of power. But it was short-lived. What looked like Satan's greatest hour became God's greatest victory. The tables were dramatically turned as Jesus burst forth from that grave on the first day of the week. Evil seemed to have the upper hand, but righteousness walked away in triumph.

We love to see the underdog come out on top. We get excited when the little guy overcomes the big obstacle. We stand and cheer when the would-be loser pulls it out in the final seconds. When Moses turns the tables and the tide on Pharaoh and prances through the Red Sea, when David downs the favored giant, or when Elijah goes toe-to-toe with the 850 false prophets, we say, "Awesome!"

We are inspired to see the great ones turning the tables, but what is even better is to turn some tables ourselves! In many of our lives Satan has his choke hold on us. Trapped in some character sin, we wonder if we will ever get free. But the tables can be turned. What looks like a stronghold of Satan can become a place of victory for God. The Spirit that turned the tables and raised Jesus from the dead lives in us (Romans 8:11)—as long as we have not become faithless, cynical or hard-hearted. Satan may have our history on his side. The momentum may be going his way. But faith in the power of God can turn the tables. Anger can be smashed; irresponsibility can be stopped; resentment can die; contentment and commitment can flourish. Our weakness can become our strength.

Ready to turn some tables? Try these seven moves:

1. **Pray**—he is listening (Hebrews 5:7).
2. **Read**—he is speaking (Luke 4:1-13).
3. **Believe**—he is able (Hebrews 2:18).
4. **Trust**—he is willing (Hebrews 4:15).
5. **Fight**—he knows what you can bear (1 Corinthians 10:13).
6. **Seek**—he has provided a way out (1 Corinthians 10:13).
7. **Find**—he gives grace in time of need (Hebrews 4:16).

Jesus' death turned the tables on Satan. The cross today is the symbol of God's victory and the reminder that the prince of this world will be driven out. When Jesus was *"lifted up from the earth"* we were drawn to him.

Now pick out your "table." Write it down, share it with others and with God's help, go turn it. Remember the cross! Take what looks like a stronghold for Satan, and turn it into a victory for God.

FOR FURTHER STUDY

Genesis 50:15-21
Daniel 3
1 Corinthians 15:50-58
2 Corinthians 2:10-11
Ephesians 6:10-18

Prayer and Purpose

Kay McKean
Sterling, Virginia

> Jesus went out as usual to the Mount of Olives, and his disciples followed him. On reaching the place, he said to them, "Pray that you will not fall into temptation." He withdrew about a stone's throw beyond them, knelt down and prayed, "Father, if you are willing, take this cup from me; yet not my will, but yours be done."
>
> —Luke 22:39-42

Thank God that Jesus was willing to "drink the cup"! Because of this, we are able to be freed from sin. We have a new life and a relationship with the Father. Jesus prayed for the Father's will to be done through him; therefore, we are able to have communion with the Father. It is because of the cross that we are able to pray. It is by looking at Christ's humble submission to the cross that we can learn *how to pray*.

Our Savior lived a sinless life, took our sins upon himself and was nailed to the cross. Without the cross, there would forever be a barrier between mankind and God the Father—the barrier of sin. But because the barrier was broken down, we can approach God with confidence, knowing that God hears us and answers our prayers through the blood of his Son. Each time we bow before the Father, we must remind ourselves *why* we are able to pray and thank God for the incredible opportunity that we have to talk to him because of his grace.

Not only does the cross give us the opportunity to pray, it also shows us the *attitude* we must have as we follow Christ in prayer. Before Jesus was crucified, it was crucial that he was reminded, through prayer, of his mission on this earth. It was not an easy mission; rather, it was one that caused him much agony and grief. How much easier if the Father would "take the cup" away from him so that he would not have to suffer. Yet, as Jesus knelt before the Father, he was able to resolve his own turmoil and have the right perspective on his suffering. The will of the Father was to save all sinners, and if that meant that Jesus had to go to the cross, he was willing to do so.

We see, as well, the example of Jesus in calling others to pray with him and for him. Jesus took his disciples with him and asked them to pray. Unfortunately, Jesus' disciples let him down by falling asleep. Jesus admonished them to "watch and pray" but also acknowledged their human limitations—"The spirit is willing, but the body is weak" (Mark 14:38). He knew how important it was for the disciples, themselves troubled and doubtful, to have a spiritual perspective and to receive strength from God. After Jesus prayed, he was able to face the mock trial, the jeering and beatings, and the crucifixion itself with a dignity and strength that amazed all who witnessed this event. Meanwhile, the disciples, who themselves had failed to pray, fled in fear and desperation. They were powerless to maintain the convictions they had so adamantly proclaimed just hours earlier!

When we kneel at the foot of the cross, we can appreciate the privilege it is to be able to pray to God. If, as disciples, we would recall this simple fact each time we begin to pray, it would radically change our prayer lives! How can we approach God with a complaining spirit or daydream and become distracted in our prayers when we realize that prayer is a privilege that we have at the cost of Jesus' death on the cross? Is praying a chore for you? Has it become boring? Remember what Jesus had to go through in order for us to be able to pray, and then you'll be inclined to pray more thoughtfully and thankfully.

Prayer with our eyes fixed on the cross enables us to have the right *perspective* on the situations troubling our hearts and minds. Often I have found myself coming to God with many anxieties and concerns. As I pray and am reminded of Jesus' prayer in the Garden of Gethsemane, God helps me to see things from his point of view. I am reminded that he is in control, that he cares for me, and that I must seek to do his will, not my own. It's incredible to know the peace that God gives as a result of praying like this! I'm so thankful that I can have God's perspective on my own life and on the situations I encounter daily.

The *purpose* of Jesus' prayer was to make sure that we could be saved. He knew that in a few short hours he would be facing mockery, physical and emotional abuse, and worst of all, crucifixion—physical and spiritual separation from God the Father. His prayer was one that rose out of intense anguish. The first Christians also had this purpose in prayer. In the midst of growth, persecution or crises, the disciples prayed for boldness and for the salvation of others. As we examine our prayer life, do we see a similar purpose? Of course God wants us to *"cast all our anxieties on him"* (1 Peter 5:7), but check to make sure that your conversation with God is centered on helping others to find him. Are you wrestling in prayer for friends that are lost? Are you asking God to help your brothers and sisters be steadfast? Jesus' purpose was to seek and save the lost; our purpose is to seek and save the lost. This purpose will blossom in prayers for the salvation of souls.

Prayer is impossible without the cross of Jesus Christ. Let us always be grateful for the *privilege* of prayer, for the perspective we receive through prayer, and for the purpose we have as we pray.

FOR FURTHER STUDY

Mark 1:32-35
Luke 22:39-46
John 17
Hebrews 4:14-16, 5:7-8,
13:15-16
Revelation 5:8, 8:4

I Am Not Alone

Thomas Marks
Westminster, Colorado

"You believe at last!" Jesus answered. "But a time is coming, and has come, when you will be scattered, each to his own home. You will leave me all alone. Yet I am not alone, for my Father is with me."

John 16:31-32

"Stress"...catch-word of the modern world! Everybody seems to have too much of it. And almost everybody has his own idea about how to get rid of it. Sociologists, psychologists and other-ologists are making a mint from it. But it's still there! It grows like a weed. It follows us everywhere; even our de-stressing attempts create stress! Studies show that vacationing often causes more stress than it relieves. So, how does a disciple deal with stress?

Let's look at Jesus. Let's go to the cross. If anybody had a reason to be stressed-out, Jesus was that person. The day of his execution could be ranked as the all-time stressful day of world history. One of his "loyal" Twelve betrays him, another denies having known him, and the other ten take flight at the mention of pain!

With this in mind, one would expect to find the gospel accounts laden with references to stress. And yet, not once is the word "stress" or any of its many synonymical cousins—worry, frustration, impatience, etc.—used to describe our Lord! Perhaps he was never tempted in the same way that we are. Maybe he can't relate to what we go through. Not at all! *"But we have one [Jesus] who has been tempted in every way, just as we are—yet was without sin"* (Hebrews 4:15).

What gave Jesus this ability? How did he conquer stress? Look again at the theme verse (John 16:31-32). Jesus understood that he was not alone. Having a partner makes all the difference. Be it in sports, academics or love itself, we were created to work in harmony with others. We all know the feeling of courage when someone stands at our side. *"Yet I am not alone, for my Father is with me."* Jesus said this a few hours before his death. Yes, stress overcame the disciples, and they all scattered, but our Lord stood firm and did not give in.

Allowing stress to overwhelm us is sin. It's giving in to the demons that want us to focus on ourselves. It's letting ourselves go. It's letting our emotions instead of convictions lead us. It's making excuses for our sin. It's running away from the responsibilities that we carry. It's not being like Jesus.

Let's look more closely at two of stress' cousins, both children of Satan:

Worry. What a wicked stress-demon! Worry consumes us. Worry makes us sick. Psychosomatic illness is well documented. The hospitals of the world are literally full of people sick with anxiety-related diseases. Our 9-year-old son, Ben, is already feeling the temptation to worry. He's anxious about whether or not his grades are good enough for university entrance! We pray often that this ugly demon would flee and never return. God answers prayer, enabling Ben to go to school full of confidence and convinced of God's presence. He understands: *"I am not alone."* Adults, take note. There will always be a thousand reasons to worry, and God will always call it sin!

Frustration. We plan and things don't go right. There's always more to do than we have time for. We spend lots of money on extravagant time-management systems and still can't get it all done. We re-examine our priorities several times a day but end up doing even less. And then it hits us—frustration. Years ago I gave several time-management seminars emphasizing methods, charts and clever plans. After 12 years in the full-time ministry, mastering a second language, adapting to a new culture, and raising three children, I have learned the secret of not getting frustrated—faith. Let me put it this way: Better to be faithful, running your life from a scrap piece of paper, than to have a fancy time-management system and be constantly living in the sin of being stressed out. My wife, children and ministry are praising God that I've gained this conviction and realize: *"I am not alone.*"

The demon the world calls "stress" must be fully driven out! Worry, frustration, impatience, anger and other stress relatives can be dealt with. It's a matter of faith—of imitating Jesus on the day of his crucifixion. Jesus prayed for strength not to give in. Jesus drove out the stress-demons. God is with us just as he was with his Son. And when we fail? The cross says we can be forgiven and start again. We too can claim the victory over stress and over sin. "*I am not alone, for my Father is with me.*"

FOR FURTHER STUDY

Romans 8:28-39
2 Corinthians 1:3-11, 4:7-12
Philippians 4:4-7
Hebrews 13:5-6
1 Peter 5:6-11

RESURRECTION

Never Forget

JANET MARKS
Westminster, Colorado

Remember Jesus Christ, raised from the dead.

—2 Timothy 2:8

I say it several times a day—don't forget. "Don't forget to make your bed." "Don't forget to say thank you." "Don't forget to get your homework done." As a mother, I constantly remind my children of the tasks at hand. I make mental notes to myself, "Don't forget that birthday card; don't forget to buy bread; don't forget; don't forget; don't forget." Remembering is not easy. God, in his wisdom, foresaw our tendency to forget. Consider how often he had to remind the Israelites not to be afraid. Think about how many memorials and feasts he set up just to help them remember his wonders. Jesus had to remind the disciples time and again to have faith. Paul and others wrote letters reminding the Christians that the cross and the resurrection were real.

I am so thankful for God's plan to help his people remember the significant events of all time: the cross and the resurrection of Jesus. How many times have we been able to take part in the communion service, only to be reminded of how little those powerful events have been on our minds? And yet each time we eat the bread and drink the wine, we are brought back to that very event. What a wondrous plan from God—just to keep us remembering.

So, what should we remember? What does the resurrection really mean to us?

New Life. *"We were therefore buried with him through baptism into death in order that, just as Christ was raised from the dead through the glory of the Father, we too may live a new life"* (Romans 6:4). Jesus threw off the shackles of death and came up from that grave not to give us a nice religious life but to lead us to something radically new and different. Having been a Christian for many years, I sometimes feel the longings for a comfortable lifestyle. The children are heading off to school; the house and the yard need attention. The idealism of my youth is waning; my energy is not what it was—WHAT? Jesus did not rise again to build a comfortable church. The death he died was one of extreme sacrifice, and then he rose to a triumphant life. Our experience should be no different. We must be ready to sacrifice all for him and to lead a life full of triumph for God. Our lives will then be characterized by consistent, heart-moving times with God, serious repentance of sin, constant concern for the lost, and a deep, abiding love for each other. There was nothing lukewarm about the resurrection.

Eternal Life. *"He has given us new birth into a living hope through the resurrection of Jesus Christ from the dead and into an inheritance that can never perish, spoil or fade, kept in heaven for you, who through faith are shielded by God's power"* (1 Peter 1:3-5). There is nothing that compares with the joy of knowing we are going to heaven and bringing others along! Knowing I have taken part in Jesus death, burial and resurrection, I have confidence that God has placed his seal on me: the promised Holy Spirit! He is the deposit guaranteeing our inheritance (Ephesians 1:13-14).

We know we will be with God eternally. Any price we pay now is well worth it, because, *"No eye has seen, no ear has heard, no mind has conceived what God has prepared for those who love him"* (1 Corinthians 2:9).

Standing alone, the crucifixion would have stopped us cold in our tracks. It would have been empty and confusing. But three days later there was a resurrection that transformed a cross into triumph. And now it transforms our old ways of thinking and living into new ones and reminds us that we will be with God forever.

"Jesus Christ raised from the dead." Don't forget. In the midst of pain, confusion, trial or challenge don't forget. Don't ever forget.

FOR FURTHER STUDY

Isaiah 53:10-11

Romans 8:5-11

1 Corinthians 15

1 Peter 1:1-9, 3:18-22

Not Surprised By Joy

JEANIE SHAW
Boston, Massachusetts

> Let us fix our eyes on Jesus, the author and perfecter of our faith, who for the joy set before him endured the cross, scorning its shame, and sat down at the right hand of the throne of God. Consider him who endured such opposition from sinful men, so that you will not grow weary and lose heart.
>
> —Hebrews 12:2-3

Jesus was a joyful person. But joy at the foot of the cross? It seems rather improbable. How can you be joyful when circumstances seem to be deteriorating right before your eyes? When health and prosperity abound and when family and friends are treating you well, it's not so hard to be happy. But when times are tough, joy can seem elusive.

As we go to the foot of the cross and fix our eyes on Jesus, we understand the secret of true joy. On the cross Jesus was rejected by many "friends." Instead of health, he experienced suffering and death. As for prosperity, lots were cast for the shirt on his back. In fact, at the cross it seemed that everything was going wrong. Jesus was being mocked and murdered. His life was ending not in glory, but in shame. No "legions of angels" came down to save the day. Yet joy was still in the heart of Jesus because he knew that God was in control and that his life would somehow bring glory to God and hope to us. He didn't argue with God. He didn't need to explain it all as he said his last few words. He didn't need to defend or justify himself to the crowd for the terrible injustices he had received. The

Scriptures say that he entrusted himself to the one who judges justly (1 Peter 2:23).

When we try to take over God's role and insist on having everything figured out, we end up putting him on trial and standing in judgment of God himself. There is no joy in

that posture.

For Jesus, there was a joy-producing freedom and peace in his acceptance of God's plan and protection. He knew he would have eternal fellowship with his Father in heaven and that all the trouble and pain we experience is not even worth comparing to what God has prepared for us (2 Corinthians 4:17).

Throughout the last days of Jesus' life on earth, he prayed for his disciples to have the full measure of his joy (John 17:13). Jesus was a joyful person. Jesus was able to look beyond the day's circumstances with an eternal and hopeful perspective. He trusted his Father.

What does this mean for you and me? When you don't understand circumstances happening around you, do you trust God, really? Or do you constantly question and sit in judgment of him? I've never met a truly happy person who tried to stand in God's place. Such a person becomes bitter and cynical. We cannot find joy trying to be something we were never meant to be.

Do you understand that Jesus is aware of and cares about your situation? He is able to work all things together for good. Even the violent scene of the cross brought about my hope and salvation. Do you understand that Jesus is preparing an eternal place for you where there is no sorrow or pain?

When I trust the fact that God is in control of my life and that he does not "mess up" in his plan for me, I do have a joyful perspective on life. When I do not trust God, I become anxious and critical.

One of our daughters has an illness that has caused her to be sick for many days over a two year period. When either of us is tempted to blame God or to feel sorry for ourselves, we lose our joy and settle into depression. This trial has not been pleasant to undergo, but I know God is strengthening her character and will use all things to his glory. She has learned to be thankful for God's many blessings—on the sick days and the well days.

Thankfulness springs from a trusting heart and gives birth to joy. You choose how you will fill your heart and mind. You can choose to be a thankful person or you can choose to keep a mental and verbal list of all the people and things you don't like. When I feel depleted of joy, I decide to be thankful to God, praying a prayer of thanksgiving until I'm happy. When I focus on being thankful, happiness is not far behind. Ask God to fill you with joy. Joy is a fruit of the Spirit, and he longs to fill you with it as you trust in God (Romans 15:13).

The joy of Jesus' relationship with God and the joy of his mission for others enabled him to endure the cross. He pushed through the cross, trusting God and knowing that our salvation was on the other side. Isaiah 53:11 says, *"After the suffering of his soul, he will see the light of life and be satisfied."*

Even the cross did not keep Jesus from being joyful. What will you allow to steal your joy? Are you rationalizing? Excusing your lack of joy? Blaming it on circumstances in your life? Fix your eyes on Jesus. He will teach you to trust and to be thankful, and in so doing, to find true joy. May you, too, see the light of life.

FOR FURTHER STUDY

Job 6:10
Psalm 5:11, 19:8, 28:7, 51:12
John 15:11, 16:20-22, 17:13
Romans 8:18,14:17
2 Corinthians 8:2
1 Thessalonians 1:6
James 1:2

Consumed With Reconciliation

Bob Tranchell
Hyannis, Massachusetts

> For he himself is our peace, who has made the two one and has destroyed the barrier, the dividing wall of hostility, by abolishing in his flesh the law with its commandments and regulations. His purpose was to create in himself one new man out of the two, thus making peace, and in this one body to reconcile both of them to God through the cross, by which he put to death their hostility.
>
> —Ephesians 2:14-16

What happens after thousands of years of people living alienated from God? Just look around. The progressing depravity that we are experiencing is the natural result of a people separated from the Creator. This alienation of man from God is transferred into man's interpersonal relationships as well. Prejudice, hatred and divorce are all manifestations of man's broken relationship with God. And where is God's heart amidst all this alienation? Does he care? The Bible makes it clear that he is, and always will be, consumed with reconciliation. From the time that Adam and Eve broke the bond with him, God has desired nothing less than reconciliation with every human being. The cross is the greatest demonstration of, as well as the effecting agent of, that desire. The reconciliation found at the foot of the cross is twofold: It first reconciles us to God, and then it reconciles us to each other.

In order for reconciliation to occur in any relationship, there must be humility on both sides. Pride, the opposite of humility, usually manifests itself in the form of fault finding. We find ourselves unable to reconcile because we are more concerned with finding fault in each other than with reconciliation. In no aspect of God's immutable character did he need to be personally humble, but he chose an incredibly humble path for Christ to travel in order to reconcile man to himself. *"Your attitude should be the same as that of Christ Jesus: Who, being in very nature God, did not consider equality with God something to be grasped, but made himself nothing, taking the very nature of a servant, being made in human likeness. And being found in appearance as a man, he humbled himself and became obedient to death—even death on a cross!"* (Philippians 2:5-8). There is no story or analogy that sufficiently describes the humility held in the heart of Christ as he walked with fallen man, only to be rejected, insulted, spat on and ultimately hung on a cross in relentless torment until he died. The heart of Christ through it all was consumed with a desire to see man reconciled. If Christ were concerned with finding fault with man, he never would have gone to the cross. The words, *"Father, forgive them for they know not what they do,"* * show how Christ was consumed with reconciliation rather than fault finding. All of this was done to put man in a position that would allow him to reach out to God and, in complete humility, find his salvation.

Man's problem is that he refuses to be humble toward God. Even though God has dramatically demonstrated humility, man is consumed with finding fault with God rather than seeing his own sin. The popular stance these days is to question and therefore, to reject God rather than question ourselves. Man cries out saying: "Why is there suffering in the world? How could a good God allow this to happen? Why didn't God stop this tragedy? How could God send someone to hell?" This is man in his pride finding fault with God and ultimately insinuating that, if given the chance, he could do a better job. This self-exaltation, better known as humanism, not only destroys man's interpersonal relationships but also destroys any hope for man to be united to God. Man's challenge is to see the humility of the cross and to humble himself before God, seeing the error of his ways and having a heart that is solely consumed with being reconciled to God. When the humility of God meets a man or woman of humility, reconciliation occurs!

In seeing what it took to unite man to God, we get an idea of what our mindset should be if we find ourselves alienated from a brother or sister. The body of Christ, the church, is made up of thousands upon thousands of imperfect human beings who find themselves sinning before God and man. God is quick to forgive; man, however, many times is not. Whether the problem is between spouses, roommates, dating couples or just members, when a division occurs, a "cross" perspective on life is needed.

Some years ago I flew into Los Angeles from Bangkok to reconcile a relationship that was divided. My attitude at the time was that I would help the brother see his fault, and we could go home united. During the counseling I was challenged that I was more concerned with being right than with being reconciled. I had spent the first session letting the other person know what he did wrong. When I admitted fault, I found myself adding "but that's because you did…" (When you place a "but" in a confession of an attitude or a sin, you are essentially saying that your sin is somebody else's fault.) When we both changed and had the attitude that we were going to be reconciled, we came together quickly. The fact was that we had both made mistakes in the relationship. Each of us needed to look at his own faults rather than the other's.

Do you really want to resolve a conflict in a relationship and do it God's way? Start with a fresh look at the cross, and remind yourself of the humility shown by Christ. Realize that if you are unwilling to humble yourself before someone, you really don't want to be reconciled with them. Make a decision that reconciliation is going to be more important to you than anything else. Take on the attitude of 1 Corinthians 6:7 which says, "Why not be wronged or even cheated rather than lose a relationship or have a conflict in the body?" When talking to the person, express your hurts; but more importantly, confess your sin in the situation. Above all, we must develop the "I would rather be reconciled than right" attitude if we are going to see the kind of unity God calls for. If, as Christians, we can keep the cross before us when there is a conflict, we will be able to keep relationships in the body united. Then together we can get on with evangelizing a depraved and needy world.

God was consumed with reconciliation—even when it took death on a cross. Are you also passionate about reconciliation—even when it means humbling yourself before God and before others?

FOR FURTHER STUDY

Matthew 5:23-24
1 Corinthians 6:1-11
Galatians 6:1-2
Ephesians 4:31-32
1 Peter 1:22-23

UNITY

Level-Ground—United Hearts

Wyndham Shaw
Boston, Massachusetts

> His purpose was to create in himself one new man out of the two, thus making peace, and in this one body to reconcile both of them to God through the cross, by which he put to death their hostility.
>
> —Ephesians 2:15-16

God wants his people united. That message is clear throughout the Bible. Unity, or the lack of it, has an immense impact on all our lives and the lives of all the significant people around us. At the cross God dramatically shows us how far he will go to produce unity.

Even in unrighteous circumstances, men have great power in unity. God noted, as the people built the tower of Babel, that with unity nothing that they planned would be impossible for them (Genesis 11:6). This is a tremendous incentive for unity in noble plans like world evangelism! Jesus declared in John 17:20-26 that unity among his disciples would be the distinctive evidence to the world that he was sent from God—in stark contrast to our present Catholic, Protestant and denominational divisions. If a house is divided against itself, Jesus taught that it cannot stand (Mark 3:25). This prophecy is fulfilled again and again by failed marriages that were never united by biblical convictions and faith. *"Make every effort,"* Paul writes, *"to keep the unity of the Spirit"* (Ephesians 4:3). Do we understand that unity is a God-given priority and provision that is emotionally and eternally vital to us all? Do we understand that at the cross God was seeking to destroy every barrier and every obstacle to unity, teaching us the love that binds everything together in perfect harmony (Colossians 2:2, 3:14)?

Rodney King, the central figure in the 1992 racial unrest in Los Angeles, asked a question the world stopped to ponder: "Can we all get along?" At the cross, God answered that question with a resounding Yes! He provided the way for us to put to death the hostility that divides us at every functional and emotional level.

But think for a minute about the obstacles to unity, and think how the attitudes we learn at the cross confront them all. Joshua 22 tells of the Israelite tribes nearly annihilating each other because of *misunderstanding* and *wrong assumptions* about their battles. It is easy to assume the worst and fail to check out our communication with those to whom we should be united. At the cross we learn to lay down our lives for each other, not jump to conclusions.

In Matthew 20:20-28, the *selfish ambition* of James and John (or at least their mother) creates disunity among the disciples. Wanting to be "the greatest" for selfish reasons will always create a competitive spirit rather than unity. At the cross we learn to *"do nothing out of selfish ambition"* (Philippians 2:4) but to consider others better than ourselves.

Inferiority and *insecurity* also create obstacles to unity, and unaddressed by the cross, lead to pulling out of or quitting the church; this is as damaging to the unity of any group as superiority or conceit. But didn't Jesus go to the cross for us all? Aren't we all equally in need of his grace and equally blessed by his justification?

The brothers of Joseph in Genesis 37 show how *jealousy and selfishness* can destroy the unity of a family or any relational unit.

The older brother in the parable of the prodigal son (Luke 15) demonstrates how *ingratitude* and *not forgiving* results in criticism instead of celebrating reunion with those we love. But can you keep such attitudes in your heart while standing at the foot of the cross?

The Bible says, *"How good and pleasant it is when brothers live together in unity"* (Psalm 133:1). Perhaps it goes without saying how painful and discouraging it is when these obstacles to unity rob us of joy in our own relationships! But the cross is God's answer for them all.

With his blood and example, Jesus provides the forgiveness needed *by us* and *from us* for unity with family, friends and brothers and sisters in Christ. Peace can replace hurt and hostility because of the love and forgiveness of the cross. Is there an ingredient more vital to unity than forgiveness? Sin is the ultimate cause of all disunity. Forgiveness is the ultimate cure. At the cross Jesus cried out, "Father, forgive them for they do not know what they are doing" (Luke 23:34). Do you realize that some of those who nailed Jesus to the cross may have later been united with him and with every Christian because of his forgiving spirit and the blood they caused to flow on Calvary? In fact, all disciples were guilty of his blood but are now perfectly united with him because of forgiveness.

Jesus' forgiveness is the key to unity, and it challenges all of our hearts. It defies our human nature, which is bent toward bitterness and vengeance rather than compassion and forgiveness. It reflects a surrender that trusts God's justice and does not take it into our own hands. It demonstrates a humility that cares less for one's own rights than for the good of others.

But have you noticed that unity is not a permanent state that one achieves? Unity is a state of being that must be continuously renewed. My wife and I have a strong, loving marriage. But our unity is threatened daily and must be renewed each time sin is committed against each other. My impatience or anger can break the spiritual and emotional oneness that God has given us. "I forgive you" is the powerful tool of the cross that puts it back together. Jesus could forgive those who unjustly crucified him and soften the heart of the very centurion who carried out his death. Who do you need to forgive totally? A friend? A wife? A husband? A child? A parent? A brother or sister in the Lord? Forgiveness is the key to being reunited.

The challenge of unity is real for each of us and appears in many relationships. We need daily to evaluate the "state of our unions" in all directions. Do you have a clear conscience before God and man in terms of unity? Have you made every effort to secure that unity? Have you gone to the cross to find it? Unity should be the expectation we have for ourselves and all those around us. Do you refuse to accept division and disharmony because it is never God's will among disciples? The ground at the foot of the cross is level. The example and blood of Jesus provide everything we need for love and unity with all who stand there with us!

FOR FURTHER STUDY

John 17

1 Corinthians 1

Ephesians 2, 4:1-13

Philippians 2:1-18

EPILOGUE

The Incredible Cross

This is being written after months of work on this book. We earnestly desired to see it produced, but we felt inadequate to undertake the task. How does it feel to work on a book when you know that no one has ever written on a more vital subject and no one ever will? Humbling. Terrifyingly and awesomely humbling. You know that no matter how careful your preparation or even consistent your prayers, what you will produce will not truly do justice to the scope, depth and majesty of your subject. But nonetheless, you feel compelled to write, knowing that the God who worked in this incredible event can once again take human words and human weakness and do amazing things in the hearts of people.

Before the cross we stand amazed. How can one event be so rich in meaning? How can something once so repugnant and loathsome now point to solutions to every human problem? Only through the working of God could it be so.

The cross. It says almost everything there is to say. It points us inward, upward and outward. It reveals our sin, shows us the nature of God and calls us to the service of others. It cuts us to the heart, yet it heals us completely.

The cross. It challenges the complacent, yet it comforts the broken and contrite. It shows us just how dark our hearts can get, yet it reveals to us how incredibly far God will go to change us. It brings us to tears, yet it lifts us to the heights. No wonder Paul would say, *"I resolved to know nothing... except Jesus Christ and him crucified."* If you get the cross, you get it. If you miss the cross, you miss it all.

Jesus and his cross are inseparable. There have been those through the years who have tried to sever the two. Like those first-century Corinthians living in the shadow of sophisticated Athens, they become embarrassed by the cross and seek to portray Jesus apart from it. They want Jesus to be the wise man, the moral leader and even the victor, but they don't want him on the cross. What they fail to understand is that Jesus apart from his cross is no help to us. We needed far more than good teaching and wise sayings. We needed a supreme example of sacrifice. But beyond and above that, we needed a Savior. Jesus apart from his cross is no savior. Take the cross away and you have a religion of human creation, not a life and lifestyle begotten of God. Take the cross away and you have but another system born of arrogance that is destined to fail.

"The cross puts everything to the test," wrote Martin Luther. How much more powerfully and righteously we will live if we learn to ask in every situation: "What does the cross mean here?"

There are poor and needy people around me. What does the cross mean here?

Someone neglected me or hurt me. What does the cross mean here?

I had great plans, but I didn't follow through. I feel terrible about myself and discouraged about trying again. What does the cross mean here?

I spoke rashly and perhaps harshly, and there is a wall between my wife and me. What does the cross mean here?

This brother or sister has something against me, and I'm tired of dealing with it. What does the cross mean here?

I've been shown needs in the kingdom, and I've been asked to sacrifice to meet them. What does the cross mean here?

In all these situations the cross will never call you to the easiest thing but always to the right thing. Sometimes you must wrestle and struggle to understand what the cross is calling for, but it is worth all the fight to finally arrive at the cross for there you will find the very center of God's perfect will. Avoid the cross, stray from it or try to pad it, and you may very well escape some pain and satisfy some desire. But in the long run you will be hurt, others will be hurt and the Spirit of God will be grieved. You will not find a resurrection by doing a u-turn before the cross.

If we won't listen to input from those "above" us or those "beside" us or those "below" us, we aren't going to the cross. If we are demanding a certain level of performance of others before we give them our acceptance, we aren't going to the cross. If we want to know "How much is enough?" or "How much do I have to do?"

we are far from the cross. If we will only serve in certain ways and if we avoid giving to those Jesus called "the least of these," we know nothing of the cross. If we stop proclaiming his message because we are opposed or persecuted or if we dilute the message to please family members or friends, we are coming down from the cross.

The cross tests us for all we are worth. It challenges every unrighteous slice of us. It says, "Crucify your greed, your self-indulgence and every ounce of racism and prejudice in your heart." It says, "Put to death every fragment of self-righteousness and arrogance." It challenges us to the very core of our being. It assures us and comforts us, but it will not let us rest. The cross was the most proactive event in history, and it is a clarion call to us all to come off the sidelines and get into the action and give until we have nothing left to give. Jesus *"emptied himself"* the Greek literally says in Philippians 2:7. God honored him mightily as he poured himself out to the last drop.

Some of us saw the cross years ago and set about to take it up daily. We need it today every bit as much as when we first began. If we have grown: (1) we understand more than ever that we can never boast save in the cross; (2) we are more in awe of amazing grace than when we first believed; and (3) dying to self is still a challenge we know we need today as much as the first day. An advancing kingdom of God has always required leaders and many, if not most of us, who have been on the Calvary road for a while, are leading at some level. But we need to understand this: Nothing disqualifies a leader in the church or the family more quickly than getting down off the cross. Our greatest danger is that we might continue to preach it and teach it but no longer be humble before it and strive to live it.

Others who are reading this have only just begun. More recently, you have seen the cross clearly for the first time. You have understood your sin that put Jesus there and the grace that covered that sin. You saw what was done for you, what it could mean to you, and how you needed to respond. And, thank God, you did respond. In repentance and baptism you came to the cross and found its power just like those 3,000 men and women baptized within days of the event itself. Hopefully, what you have read here has taken you even deeper. But our prayer is that what you have read has made you even more aware of how much more you can learn. Hopefully, it has opened your eyes to how wide and deep and long and high is the love of God. Hopefully, it has clarified for you the way that love beckons you to follow Jesus Christ. If you heard these things with an open and tender heart, they have deepened your gratitude and strengthened your determination to take up the cross daily and never, ever turn back.

Whether we have been coming to the cross for years or only for a few months, one fact remains: We need each other as we take it up. The church is the community of the cross, and everything about the cross calls us into each other's lives. No one misunderstands the message as much as the person who says, "I want the cross, but I'll go it alone." *"This is how we know what love is: Jesus Christ laid down his life for us. And we ought to lay down our lives for our brothers"* (1 John 3:16).

Let us, then, unite at the foot of the cross and together find the joy of living it and sharing it with the whole world. Nothing else will do.

—Tom A. Jones

When I survey the wondrous cross
on which the Prince of glory died,

My richest gain I count but loss
and pour contempt on all my pride.

Forbid it, Lord, that I should boast,
save in the death of Christ, my Lord;

All the vain things that charm me most
I sacrifice them to his blood.

See, from his head, his hands, his feet,
sorrow and love flow mingled down;

Did e'er such love and sorrow meet,
or thorns compose so rich a crown?

Were the whole realm of nature mine,
that were a present far too small;

Love so amazing, so divine,
demands my soul, my life, my all.

—Isaac Watts

APPENDIX

Short Thoughts for Crucial Moments

Thoughts are powerful. Even short thoughts can have a great effect. On the following pages are short quotations taken from the articles you have just read. These are not offered as a substitute for the complete readings. There is no effort here to give a lazy man's approach to the cross. But, sometimes after you have seriously wrestled with the truth of the Scriptures and are faced with some situation, you just need a reminder, a quick jab to get your heart and mind where it needs to be. These selections are offered to meet that need.

When we stand at the foot of the cross and behold the love of God, we see how unbelievably unconditional his love is. You can lose your health, your possesions, even your reputation, and God's love for you will not be affected in the slightest....While we were sinners—in the worst of shape—God demonstrated his love for us at the cross.

—Tom A. Jones
Unconditional Love

The greater the capacity to love, the greater the capacity to feel pain. The greater the love, the greater the potential for being hurt. When it comes to the cross, it must state emphatically to us all the days of our lives—feel the pain!

—Randy McKean
Hating Sin

With greater understanding and faith in the cleansing power of Jesus' blood, what will you do the next time you are convicted of sin? Will you pull out your old, useless, self-invented sacrifices, or will you appeal to God's grace through Christ's continual atoning blood? Will you wallow in self-pity, or will you celebrate Jesus' ongoing work in your behalf?

—Marcia Lamb
The Blood of Christ

Make a firm decision to forgive, and refuse to let anything or anyone stop you from carrying out that decision. When you have truly replaced the evil with good, you will know it, for then your very soul will be flooded with a peace which transcends all understanding (Philippians 4:7).

—Theresa Ferguson
Forgiveness

When we stand at the foot of the cross and behold the love of God, we see how unbelievably unconditional his love is. You can lose your health, your possessions, even your reputation, and God's love for you will not be affected in the slightest....While we were sinners—in the worst of shape—God demonstrated his love for us at the cross.

—Roger Lamb
Baptism

Self-examination is different from self-condemnation. As we honestly take stock of our hearts, attitudes, motives and actions, we should be driven to the blood of Christ for forgiveness. There is no need for ongoing guilt or worldly sorrow. For even our tears of repentance must be washed in the blood of Christ.

—Chelly Larson
The Lord's Supper

We simply need to accept that we will never be accepted by the religious community, the intellectual world or the popular media. The message of the cross always has been and will be foolishness to those who are perishing.

—Roy Larson
Wisdom

Thanks be to God that Jesus has taken the "credit" for my prideful heart and that he has given me credit for his righteousness. The reckoning miracle of the cross. Therefore, all credit for my own righteousness is his.

—Sheila Jones
Boasting

Surrender, or death to self, is an emotional break with self in control. We become willing to yield our lives, our health, our family, our finances, our future and our plans totally to him. We are willing to accept what we need rather than stubbornly to insist on what we want. In essence, we allow God to be God in our daily lives.

—Gordon Ferguson
Surrender

When introduced to Jesus Christ, we are attracted by his love, his inspiration and his care for others. He calls us to imitate him, and that is exciting. But there is no way to love and serve others as Jesus did and avoid denying ourselves. Any limitation we put on self-denial will surely limit our usefulness to him and the way God can bless us.

—Javier Amaya
Self-Denial

Jesus was a man of passion, purpose and deep convictions. He embraced his task, confronted his opponents, and pressed on resolutely toward his goal. He was no wimp, but he was humble. He was humble on the road to the cross, and he was humble the day he went to the cross.

—Tom Franz
Humility

Making the cross your lifestyle means dealing quickly with sin. It means admitting sin to yourself and confessing it to God and others. It means repenting quickly and not letting sin drag on for days or even weeks. God wants each of us to have a joy-filled, abundant life that is full of impact. Does that describe your life?

—Carol McGuirk
Lifestyle

Biblical sacrifice is taking something very valuable to you and totally giving it up because you believe that more good will come from giving it than from grasping it.

—Mary Franz
Sacrifice

God's will for Jesus' life was hard. *"It was the Lord's will to crush him and cause him to suffer"* (Isaiah 53:10), yet Jesus was never angry, resentful or rebellious toward God. He accepted God's will for his life, and in the same way we need to accept the things that happen in our lives.

—Kelly Amaya
Suffering

Nothing moves the human heart more than someone who puts the need of another above his or her own need and willingly serves. It is a rare and precious expression of love. When Jesus washed his disciples' feet, showing them the full extent of his love, they were shocked, humbled and deeply moved. He then, in turn, told them to do the same for others—to be servants. He was teaching them how to have impact.

—Maria Rogers
Serving

Jesus makes it clear that the degree of true greatness in his kingdom is determined by the degree to which one has become a bond-servant (Mark 10:35-44). Do we hear that? This greatness comes not through self-exaltation but through self-denial, with God thereby exalting one to true greatness. Do we deeply believe this?

—Doug Webber
Serving

As it was with Jesus, so it will be with you and me. We will have to fight some tough battles, but let us settle in our hearts one issue: We will never quit. We will reach our goal.

—Jimmy Rogers
Determination

But how did he get through the cruel and vicious attacks with such grace "He entrusted himself to him who judges justly" (1 Peter 2:23), and he kept his focus on the joy that would be his (Hebrews 12:2). These men didn't know what they were doing, but God did. These men were not in control. God was. These men would not win. God would. Such trust is the key to endurance in the midst of attack.

—Laurie Tranchell
Persecution

When the toughest challenges come and when being a disciple seems to be too radical, just remember that Jesus is the important person. All of our other inside connections are secondary to him. He is the Chairman of the Board.

—Dan Bathon
In the Working World

Being a Christian parent doesn't mean you try to spare your children the cross; it means you show them how to get on it. Do you teach your children that God has a plan for their lives? Do they see you sacrifice to bring them to salvation? Do they see you sacrifice your time, your worldly desires, your money, your sleep—all for the lost?

—Julie Bathon
In the Family

Are you imitating God's attitude toward sin? Do you want to blot out those useless, tiresome, sinful patterns that rob you of your joy and your power as a Christian? . . . In response to his best, decide you will give your best.

—Adrienne Scanlon
The Nature of God

The cross and the resurrection give us reasons for faith in all God's promises. At the cross Jesus shows us that faith in the most difficult moments will be rewarded.

—Joanne Webber
Faith

The world is screaming out, "Save yourself! Come down from your cross!" Jesus is crying back, "Don't come down!" What are you going to do? It will determine the eternal destiny of many others. You love people too much to come down. Make the decision Jesus did. Make it again tomorrow and the next day. And one day soon someone will thank you for not coming down.

—Brian Scanlon
Loving the Lost

Trapped in some character sin, we wonder if we will ever get free. But the tables can be turned. What looks like a stronghold of Satan can become an occasion for the victory of God. The Spirit that turned the tables and raised Jesus from the dead lives in us (Romans 8:11).

—John McGuirk
Overcoming

After Jesus prayed, he was able to face the mock trial, the jeering and beatings, and the crucifixion itself with a dignity and strength that amazed all who witnessed this event. Meanwhile, the disciples, who themselves had failed to pray, fled in fear and desperation.

—Kay McKean
Prayer

What gave Jesus this ability? How did he conquer stress?...Jesus understood that he was not alone. Having a partner makes all the difference!

—Thomas Marks
Handling Stress

Jesus Christ raised from the dead. In the midst of pain, confusion, trial or challenge, don't forget. Don't ever forget.

—Janet Marks
Resurrection

When we try to take over God's role and insist on having everything figured out, we end up putting him on trial and standing in judgment of God himself. There is no joy in that posture.

—Jeanie Shaw
Joy

Do you really want to resolve a conflict in a relationship and do it God's way? Start with a fresh look at the cross, and remind yourself of the humility shown by Christ. Realize that if you are unwilling to humble yourself before someone, you really don't want to be reconciled with them.

—Bob Tranchell
Reconciliation

Is there an ingredient more vital to unity than forgiveness? Sin is the ultimate cause of all disunity. Forgiveness is the ultimate cure. At the cross Jesus cried out, *"Father, forgive them, for they do not know what they are doing"* (Luke 23:34).

—Wyndham Shaw
Unity

Sometimes you must wrestle and struggle to understand what the cross is calling for, but it is worth all the fight to finally arrive at the cross, for there you will find the very center of God's perfect will.

—Tom A. Jones
Epilogue

www.ipibooks.com

www.ingramcontent.com/pod-product-compliance
Ingram Content Group UK Ltd.
Pitfield, Milton Keynes, MK11 3LW, UK
UKHW041823200726
13854UKWH00002BA/510

9 781948 450331